THE PRIEST OF NEMI
A PHILOSOPHICAL DRAMA (1886)

Ernest Renan

Translated from the French
with an Introduction by

Michael Eaton

Shoestring Press

1) Great Is Diana – statue of the goddess in the Ny Carlsberg Glyptotek, Copenhagen

The still glassy lake that sleeps
Beneath Aricia's trees,
Those trees in whose dim shadow
The ghastly priest doth reign,
The priest who slew the slayer
And shall himself be slain.

Thomas Babington Macaulay, *The Lays of Ancient Rome* (1842)

All rights reserved. No part of this work covered by the copyright herein may be reproduced or used in any means – graphic, electronic, or mechanical, including copying, recording, taping, or information storage and retrieval systems – without written permission of the publisher.

Printed by imprintdigital
Upton Pyne, Exeter
www.imprintdigital.net

Typeset by types of light
typesoflight@gmail.com

Published by Shoestring Press
19 Devonshire Avenue, Beeston, Nottingham, NG9 1BS
(0115) 925 1827
www.shoestringpress.co.uk

First published 2013

Translation and introduction, copyright © 2013 Michael Eaton

The moral right of the author has been asserted

Front cover image, copyright © 2013 Barrett Hodgson

ISBN 978-1-907356-69-8

CONTENTS

Introduction   xi

The Priest of Nemi

   Prologue   5

   Scene One   7

   Scene Two   26

   Scene Three   43

   Scene Four   46

   Scene Five   50

   Scene Six   59

   Scene Seven   65

   Scene Eight   68

INTRODUCTION

Nemi in Nottingham

Nottingham Castle is something of a disappointment to visitors who expect to find a fortress with towers and turrets, familiar from Robin Hood movies. The medieval royal palace was largely destroyed in the Civil War and what little remained was burnt down by our radical forebears in the Reform Bill riots of 1831. But the building has always been a place of wonder for me – not the rather nondescript ducal mansion restored in the late nineteenth century, but what was on display within. For this was the country's first municipal Museum and Art Gallery.

When I was child there was one room I found especially intriguing. It contained treasures from the Temple of Diana at Nemi, south of Rome off the Appian Way. Why was I so fascinated? These exhibits, which exerted such a powerful attraction, were not especially spectacular. Most were incomplete, broken, partial; votive offerings to a female deity who had not been worshipped for nearly two thousand years. But to see them provoked troubling thoughts. Were those adherents who flocked to this shrine to entreat the healing powers of the goddess possessed of a devotion as profound and sincere as that of the true believers who taught me their faith at Sunday School? Did the idolatrous followers of this Roman cult expect the very same kind of protection from the perils and dangers of this life as those worshippers of the Christian faith which supplanted hers? Whose prayers were answered?

These artefacts are no longer on open display, as they were when I was growing up. Today the wondrous remnants of the cult of Diana are safely wrapped in storage until, it is to be hoped, they will soon find a permanent home where they might once again perplex and confound the minds of another generation.

I could never have imagined that, half a century later, I would be allowed rare and privileged access into this sacred site, which remains in private ownership near the town of Ariccia in the Alban Hills; that I would see for myself the sylvan grove by the glassy lake; that I would enter the sanctified surrounds of the Priest of Nemi. Nor did it occur to me to wonder why such magical objects from a pagan Roman temple might be on display in a museum in my home town in the English Midlands.

Only later was I to learn that this significant archaeological site had been excavated in the mid-1880s by Sir John Savile Lumley (later Lord Savile) whose family seat was at Rufford Abbey in Nottinghamshire. While serving as Ambassador in Rome he obtained permission from the landowner, Prince Orsini, to search for the temple at Nemi, the precise location of which was unknown following its complete destruction by a landslide sometime in the second century CE. Though very much an amateur in the Victorian mould, Savile was nevertheless a serious, competent archaeologist and his excavation did, indeed, uncover the sanctuary. The arrangement the British diplomat had made with the Italian aristocrat allowed the Prince to keep half of whatever was uncovered on his property. So it was that Orsini duly creamed off those items he considered the most precious of the spoils for quick sale, dispersing them into the international art market.

Savile's remaining fifty percent of the finds has proved crucial for study of the religious practices performed at the temple by the lake which was known as *speculum Dianae*, Diana's Mirror. She, whom the Greeks called upon as Artemis and whose earlier counterpart must have been worshipped in a name unknown by the native peoples of Latium, was the stern, chaste 'goddess of many parts.' Diana presided over hunting, healing, childbirth, the moon and even, in one of her guises, the underworld: she was known as *trivia*, deity of the hallowed ground where three roads meet, propitiated by barren wives and women in childbirth, the especial object of veneration by slaves. The votives unearthed at Nemi provide an insight into the practice of Roman religion and the belief of pilgrims who visited her sanctuary more valuable than the costly marble statues Prince Orsini might have filched and flogged off.

Savile generously donated his findings to a museum which belongs to the people of Nottingham. So thanks to this munificent ambassador I have always considered myself to be a proud part-owner of this important classical collection.

Nemi in *The Golden Bough*

If antiquarian relics in a small room off a staircase in a provincial museum sowed the first seeds of doubt then the death knell finally tolled a few years later when I read *The Golden Bough* by James Frazer. The Sea of Faith had never been so turbulent.

Perhaps despite his own best intentions, this great Scottish classicist, son of a devout Glaswegian pharmacist, must have been responsible for setting more seekers off on journeys down the rocky road to agnosticism than anyone since Darwin. How could a reader of Frazer's accounts of the mysteries of the ancient Near East – the ritual dramas of Attis, Adonis and Osiris – fail to perceive implicit structural similarities between the mythical tales of these heathen supernatural beings, who died only to rise again, and the central narrative of the Christian faith?

In the early years of the twentieth century Frazer's impact was all-pervasive, not only upon modernist writers and classicists but also among the thinking populace at large. Did he welcome T.S. Eliot's famous valediction in the Notes to *The Waste Land*, that '*The Golden Bough* has influenced our generation profoundly'? What did the conservative scholar make of Sigmund Freud's idiosyncratic use of this work to bolster his own grim fairy-tale of human history's foundation by a primal horde slaughtering (and eating) their father? He would certainly have reacted with pride to the assessment of his Cambridge contemporary, the Hellenist Jane Harrison, when she wrote that Frazer lit 'the dark wood of savage superstition with a gleam from *The Golden Bough* ... the scales fell – we heard and understood.' But perhaps he would have been troubled to hear her anecdote, recounted in the Preface to *Themis*, Harrison's Frazerian **S***tudy Of The Social Origins Of Greek Religion*: 'A cultured policeman ... whom I was privileged to entertain at Cambridge, said to me, "I used to believe everything they told me, but, thank God, I read *The Golden Bough* and I've been a freethinker ever since."'

This all but mythological policeman was not alone. The work had a similarly corrosive effect on my own teenage self.

Frazer's monument progressed through ever-changing and ever-expanding editions: two volumes on first publication in 1890; growing to three with smaller type-face in 1900; increasing to no fewer than twelve weighty annotated tomes for the definitive Third Edition which came out between 1911 and 1915; then appearing in the best-selling abridged form (still about 800 pages) in 1922, before a final volume, an 'Aftermath', was published in 1936 long after the work's best-before date. This book, in one form or another, was once on a shelf in every well-read household. It has never been out of print since its first appearance, so somebody somewhere must still be buying, if not reading, *The Golden Bough*.

Frazer's theories developed and transformed over the decades of this voluminous expansion, evidenced by the change of emphasis in his subtitle from a 'Study in Comparative Religion' to a 'Study of Magic and Religion'. Nevertheless, in every subsequent revision, the work always started and ended with an account of a barbaric ritual enacted in a distant yet, to me, all too familiar site... where but in those wooded precincts of the Temple of Diana, the very place where the votive objects which so fascinated me as a child had been discovered!

Once again I was transported to Nemi:

> No one who has seen the woodland lake of Nemi – 'Diana's Mirror' as it was called by the ancients – can ever forget it. That calm water, lapped in a green hollow of the Alban hills... Dian herself might still linger by this lonely shore, still haunt these woodlands wild... Here, in the very heart of the wooded hills, the goddess Diana had an old and famous sanctuary, the resort of pilgrims from all parts of Latium. It was known as the sacred grove of *Diana Nemorensis*: Diana of the Wood, a fitting home for the 'mistress of mountains and forests green and lonely glades and sounding rivers' as Catullus calls her.
>
> The great wealth and popularity of the sanctuary in antiquity are attested by ancient writers as well as by the remains which have come to light in modern times. It was reputed to be one of the richest in Italy. The abundance of cheap votive offerings and copper coins, which the site has yielded in our own day, speaks volumes for the piety and numbers, if not for the opulence and liberality, of the worshippers. Swarms of beggars used to stream forth daily from the slums of Aricia and take their stand on the long slope up which the labouring horses dragged well-to-do pilgrims to the shrine; and, according to the response which their whines and importunities met with, they blew kisses or hissed curses after the carriages as they swept rapidly down hill again.

What made this temple of particular interest for Frazer, though, was not the pilgrims who visited it but the Priest who presided over it:

> In antiquity this sylvan landscape was the scene of a strange and recurring tragedy. Dark crimes were often perpetrated there under the mask of religion, crimes which after the lapse of so many ages still lend a touch of melancholy to these quiet woods and waters, like a chill breath of autumn on one of

those bright September days 'while not a leaf seems faded.'

A custom was observed there which seems to transport us at once from civilisation to savagery. In the sacred grove there grew a certain tree round which at any time of the day, and probably far into the night, a grim figure might be seen to prowl. In his hand he carried a drawn sword, and he kept peering warily about him as if at every instant he expected to be set upon by an enemy. He was a priest and a murderer; and the man for whom he looked was sooner or later to murder him and hold the priesthood in his stead. Such was the rule of the sanctuary. A candidate for the priesthood could only succeed to office by slaying the priest, and having slain him, he retained office till he was himself slain by a stronger or a craftier.

The post which he held by this precarious tenure carried with it the title of *Rex Nemorensis*: 'King of the Wood'; but surely no crowned head ever lay uneasier, or was visited by more evil dreams, than his. For year in year out, in summer and winter, in fair weather and in foul, he had to keep his lonely watch, and whenever he snatched a troubled slumber it was at the peril of his life. The least relaxation of his vigilance, the smallest abatement of his strength of limb or skill of fence, put him in jeopardy; grey hairs might seal his death-warrant.

To gentle and pious pilgrims at the shrine the sight of him might well seem to darken the fair landscape, as when a cloud suddenly blots the sun on a bright day. The dreamy blue of Italian skies, the dappled shade of summer woods, and the sparkle of waves in the sun, can have accorded but ill with that stern and sinister figure, pacing to and fro, now in twilight and now in gloom, a dark figure with a glitter of steel at the shoulder whenever the pale moon, riding clear of the cloud-rack, peers down at him through the matted boughs.

> Within the sanctuary at Nemi grew a certain tree of which no branch might be broken. Only a runaway slave was allowed to break off, if he could, one of its boughs. Success in the attempt entitled him to fight the priest in single combat, and if he slew him he reigned in his stead. According to the ancients the fateful branch was that Golden Bough which, at the Sibyl's bidding, Aeneas plucked before he essayed the perilous journey to the world of the dead.

When, in the 1970s, I became a student of Social Anthropology – the academic discipline of which Frazer was undoubtedly a Founding Father – I soon learned that the sons and daughters who succeeded him had, like Freud's primal horde and, indeed, not unlike the Priest of Nemi himself, sacrificed the patriarch and gobbled up his reputation. Like those Divine Kings so central to his argument, Frazer's persona had become surrounded by Taboo.

Edmund Leach, the brilliant structural anthropologist and Provost of my Cambridge college, King's, treated Frazer, both the man and the work, with particular derision. The book, which had been so important to my own adolescent development, was now dismissed by a new mentor as 'a monumental hulk of scholastic futility' and 'a paradigm of all that budding anthropologists should learn to shun.' For Leach even Frazer's prose 'evokes a sense of ridicule'.

The liberal social sciences became embarrassed by Frazer's shadow. He was dismissed as a man very much of his age who had never left his library armchair to collect data 'in the field', instead uncritically sifting through dubious reports from missionaries and colonial administrators. Furthermore, he never came to know any non-Western peoples at first-hand. 'Alas,' said Leach, 'the only 'savage' that Frazer ever encountered in the flesh was a Wild Man From Borneo in a circus tent and he found the experience very distasteful.' William James, psychologist of religious experience and brother of the more-famous Henry, met Frazer in Rome in 1900 and seems to confirm this fear of the Other for, when asked if he had ever met any 'natives' in the flesh, Frazer apparently responded: 'Heaven forbid.' He was even calumnised by Leach as something of a racist: 'Frazer's 'savage' is a lunatic at large – a child of nature whose ignorance evokes our amusement rather than our sympathy' – an unfair simplification contradicted not least by Malinowski, whom we were taught was the true 'Father of Social Anthropology'. The conventional wisdom became that Frazer's grand design and his 'comparative method' were ridiculous, erroneous, out-moded Victorian chimerae, operating from the founding principle that, again as Leach put it: 'the fundamental psychology of human beings everywhere will be reflected by similar customary behaviours, or conversely, that similar customs always have the same symbolic implications, regardless of the context in which they appear.'

So, for Frazer, rituals and beliefs occurring in one historical society or ethnological culture can be explained by reference from and analogy to rites and doctrines practised in entirely different times and/or places:

> If we can show that a barbarous custom, like that of the priesthood of Nemi, has existed elsewhere; if we can detect the motives which led to its institution; if we can prove that these motives have operated widely, perhaps universally, in human society, producing in varied circumstances a variety of institutions specifically different but generically alike; if we can show, lastly, that these very motives, with some of their derivative institutions, were actually at work in classical antiquity; then we may fairly infer that at a remoter age the same motives gave birth to the priesthood of Nemi.

Very big 'ifs' indeed. No such thing as cultural relativism for this evolutionary universalist *par excellence*.

It is not out of any desire to exonerate the author of *The Golden Bough* from largely justified, if exaggeratedly disdainful, attacks that I would defend Frazer. Though his work has become entirely marginal to the history of the anthropology it remains central to the history of ideas. Though his work can be dismissed as bad science, fallacious philosophy and undocumented history, nevertheless his status as a giant-killer remains unassailed. Today his reputation might still be reclaimed, at least partially, if (if!) he is approached not as an analyst of but as a maker of myths. Frazer was, as he himself put it in another context, 'guided by the purple glow of the Imagination.' Besides, *pace* Sir Edmund, I think he is a great prose stylist!

Perhaps the work ought to be considered as literature, a great novel of suspense with its writer as a pioneering psychological detective, employing his own patented forensic tool-kit of 'the comparative method' to solve nothing less ambitious than the riddle of the evolution of human thought and the origins of culture. And this mystery story begins nowhere else but Nemi:

> Why had Diana's priest, the King of the Wood, to slay his predecessor? And why, before doing so, had he to pluck from a certain tree, the Golden Bough?

But a further question remains: Why did Frazer settle upon this particular ritual as the starting point for his life-long quest to make sense of the weird, in his own words: 'Manners, Customs, Religion and Superstitions etc. of Uncivilized and Semi-Civilized Peoples'?

Nemi in Classical Literature

Frazer had encountered the primitive, barbaric rite of the King of the Wood in the writings of the classical authors he had studied since childhood. Among them the historian Strabo, who may even have met the incumbent of his own time, told of the runaway slave who could only gain the office of Priest by fighting his predecessor in a duel to the death. The biographer Suetonius provided a tantalisingly brief anecdote to demonstrate the psychopathic nature of one of the rulers of Rome: 'There was no man of so abject or mean condition, whose excellency in any kind Caligula did not envy. The *Rex Nemorensis* had for many years enjoyed the honour of the priesthood, so he procured a still stronger antagonist to oppose him.' The Virgilian commentator Servius added the crucial detail of a certain branch which must be discovered and broken from a specific tree in the grove before the challenge to mortal combat could be made. And it was from the Greek travel writer Pausanias (whose work Frazer translated, accompanied by a, naturally, lengthy commentary) that he derived one of the tales of the temple's fabled foundation. This is how Frazer's purple imagination retells the tale:

> Hippolytus, chaste and fair, spent all his days in the greenwood chasing wild beasts with the virgin huntress Artemis for his only comrade. Proud of her divine society, he spurned the love of women, and this proved his bane. For Aphrodite, stung by his scorn, inspired his step-mother Phaedra with love of him; and when he disdained her wicked advances she falsely accused him to his father Theseus. The slander was believed and Theseus prayed to his sire Poseidon to avenge the imagined wrong.
>
> So while Hippolytus drove in a chariot by the shore of the Saronic Gulf, the sea-god sent a fierce bull forth from the waves. The terrified horses bolted, threw Hippolytus from the chariot, and dragged him at their hoofs to death. But Diana, for the love she bore Hippolytus, persuaded Asclepius, the god of medicine, to bring her fair young hunter back to life by his simples. Diana disguised the features by adding years to his life, and then bore him far away to the dells of Nemi, to live there, unknown and solitary, under the name of Virbius, in the depth of the Italian forest.

The only artistic depiction for this mythic cycle I know of can be seen in the Locanda Martorelli in Ariccia, the stately Italian town built upon the site of the ancient Latium settlement of its almost name-sake Aricia. On the walls of this late eighteenth century palazzo, once an obligatory venue for European artists in Italy and so now known as the Museo del Grand Tour, the Polish painter Taddeo Kuntze painted a series of murals in tempera. They show in sequence: the virtuous young hero spurning the advances of his father's nubile wife; his guardian goddess seeking the aid of the god of medicine to revive her favourite after his destruction by the sea monster; the performance of a ritual of fire in the temple by the reincarnated old priest; and Diana with her female acolytes hunting the deer in the woodland.

None of the sources from antiquity, however, confirm the thread of inference upon which Frazer was to hang his thesis: that the mortal priest/king became the bridegroom of the immortal goddess; that their marital union secured the vegetative fertility of the tribal lands; that when his strength began to wane he must be ritually sacrificed and replaced by a younger, more potent heir to the office; that the sacred tree from which the challenger must break a bough was an oak and that this branch, Aeneas's Golden Bough, was mistletoe.

Frazer defused any challenge to his tentative argument, being the first to admit that 'direct evidence there is none, but analogy pleads in favour of the view.' His bamboozled battalion of readers may well have forgotten the crime by the time they arrive at the solution, unperturbed by the fact that Turner's masterpiece which provided the title of Frazer's own masterwork and which was reproduced as the frontispiece to every edition, is actually set at Lake Avernus, nowhere near Lake Nemi!

Nemi and James Frazer

Frazer didn't actually see the site at Nemi with his own eyes until after the publication of his first two editions, though he had, of course, followed the well-publicised reports of the excavations. One of Savile's discoveries was to prove particularly crucial to the development of his argument. This was a double-headed marble herm, dating from the second century CE, which had been photographed but which subsequently disappeared – perhaps it was part of Orsini's loot? Fortunately, a plaster cast was made which is still unforgettable. Frazer had a chance to examine this copy personally at the Castle Museum in 1907 whilst he was preparing the Third Edition. Might this statue represent the dread Priest of Nemi in both of his two-faced facets?

> A curious monument of the ill-fated dynasty appears to have come down to us in a double-headed bust which was found in the sanctuary at Nemi. It represents two men of heavy and somewhat coarse features and a grim expression. One is young and beardless with shut lips and a steadfast gaze, the other is a man of middle life with a tossed and matted beard, wrinkled brows, a wild anxious look in the eyes, and an open grinning mouth. But perhaps the most singular thing about the two heads are the leaves with scalloped edges which are plastered, so to say, on the necks of both busts and apparently also under the eyes of the younger figure. The leaves have been interpreted as oak leaves and this interpretation, which is not free from doubt, is confirmed by the resemblance to an oak leaf which the moustache of the older figure clearly presents when viewed in profile. If the leaves on the two heads are indeed oak we should have to conclude that the tree which the King of the Wood guarded and personated was an oak.
>
> Various explanations of this remarkable monument have been proposed; but the most probable theory appears to be that the older figure represents the priest of Nemi, the King of the Wood, in possession, while the other face is that of his youthful adversary and possible successor. This theory would explain the striking contrast between the set determined gaze

of the younger man and the haggard, scared look of the older. On the one face we seem to read the resolution to kill, on the other the fear to die.

'Various explanations … not free from doubt': quite an understatement! For few experts have concurred with the description that what surrounds these faces are even foliage, let alone leaves from the tree of an oak, an essential interpretation as connective tissue for the convoluted plot of *The Golden Bough*. The earliest account of the Nottingham cast describes these characters as 'aquatic monsters' and what emerges from their mouths is not 'leafy' but 'finny'!

I have seen two other double-headed herms from Nemi and there seems to be no consensus from connoisseurs as to who or what they might represent. One is in the Ny Carlsberg Glyptotek in Copenhagen and is all but identical to Savile's photograph – perhaps this is where the Prince's booty ended up? Here the embellishments on the 'hair, mouth and neck' of these figures are also catalogued as 'fins', leading to a speculation that these might be personifications of the *genii loci* of two lakes: Albano and Nemi. The other resides nearer its native home in the Museo del Navi near Lake Nemi and close to the temple site. In this exhibit the features of both characters, youthful and agèd, are smoother, less grotesque, far from anxious, far more settled. Here they are definitely described as depictions of the founders of the sanctuary: Hippolytus and Virbius – the Young Man reborn as the Old Priest.

Could these recent archaeological discoveries, possibly confirming the strange and uncivilised tale from the classical authors he knew so well, have stimulated Frazer to deploy the brutal drama enacted in the sacred grove as a narrative device which would provide a continuing sense of suspense to organise his bulbous study? Or could it have been a more recent literary work which lit the touch-paper of inspiration?

Could it have been Frazer's reading of an unperformed and untranslated French play, a copy of which he certainly owned, which contributed to the structural organisation of *The Golden Bough*, turning what might have been an unreadable and haphazard collection of bizarre 'customs of the world' culled from distant times and exotic places, into an intellectual adventure yarn, ensuring its future massive authority?

In his biography *J.G. Frazer – His Life and Work* Robert Ackerman makes the suggestion that the spark could have been struck by a *drame philosophe*, published in 1886, about the same time as the excavations: *Le Prêtre de Nemi* by Ernest Renan. But if this relatively unknown play did have such a crucial effect then why did Frazer never acknowledge Renan's significance? The hypothesis which follows is not theoretical but personal.

Frazer's closest friend, the colleague he always credited with widening his horizons from the well-ploughed earth of classical scholarship to the uncharted waters of the fledgling study of mankind, was William Robertson Smith. A fellow Scot, also from a background of the Free Church into which he was ordained, Robertson Smith gained unwanted notoriety whilst occupying the Chair of Hebrew in his native Aberdeen. Though remaining a devout believer, his intellectual conscience could not allow him to ignore advances coming from Germany where, as a young student, he had been exposed to a radical new form of Biblical analysis which treated the scriptures as historical texts rather than heavenly revelation. Robertson Smith's *Encyclopaedia Britannica* entry on the ' Bible' bore all the hallmarks of this Teutonic Higher Criticism, amazingly leading to his arraignment before the Free Presbytery of Aberdeen on the charge of Heresy. He was accused of: 'Publishing and promulgating opinions which contradict or are opposed to the doctrine of the immediate inspiration, infallible truth, and divine authority of the Holy Scriptures.'

Following several personally troubling and highly publicised trials Robertson Smith was eventually dismissed from his post. Fortunately, a Readership in Arabic suddenly became vacant at the University of Cambridge – the previous incumbent had been assassinated in Sinai, possibly because he was on a clandestine espionage mission! So the heretic came south to a more open-minded environment where he would meet and forge a strong bond with a young Fellow of Trinity College: James Frazer.

Still connected with the Edinburgh based encyclopaedia, which had all but scuppered his career, Robertson Smith commissioned his new-found friend to contribute a series of articles on his specialist subject, the Classics, including 'Pericles', 'Prosperpine' and 'Priapus' – the ninth edition had evidently reached the letter P. When volume T loomed, Robertson Smith, whose own work on *The Religion of the Semites* had already decisively moved far away from scriptural exegesis and into ethnological speculation, persuaded Frazer to go beyond his classical comfort zone and undertake 'Taboo' and 'Totemism.' Without ever leaving his library Frazer set off on a course which would in time make him the world's most celebrated armchair anthropologist. Small wonder that a couple of years later the first edition of *The Golden Bough* was dedicated: 'To My Friend William Robertson Smith In Gratitude And Admiration.'

What has any of this to do with *Le Prêtre de Nemi*?

Robertson Smith was completely contemptuous of Renan's scholarship. In an 1888 review of the Gallic orientalist's *Histoire du Peuple d'Israël* he dismissed the work as 'half-imaginative ... altogether wrong', a product not of sound historical reconstruction but of the author's imagination, 'divination' even. Given this condemnation Frazer could presumably not risk recognition of even the smallest debt to a French writer considered little more than a charlatan by his dearest companion to whom he owed so much.

The claim that Renan's play might well have been a *fons et origo* has been disputed by another eminent Frazerian. In *The Making of The Golden Bough – The Origins and Growth of an Argument* Robert Fraser dismisses the speculation as 'at most a small contributory factor.' But I am inclined to accept, perhaps because I want to believe, that the conjunction of Savile's archaeological discoveries at the Temple of Diana with a drama about the ancient priesthood on that very site may have provided Frazer with his founding, structuring principle.

The possibility must be admitted that *The Golden Bough* was stimulated by *Le Prêtre de Nemi*.

Nemi and Ernest Renan

There are aspects of Renan's life which have something in common with the career of Robertson Smith – providing perhaps another, less conscious, cause for the Scotsman's animosity towards his French rival? But Renan was an even greater controversialist, a far more illustrious heretic.

A Breton of modest background whose seaman father had drowned when he was a child, Renan entered a seminary to train for the priesthood, until he too came under the heady spell of Germanic Biblical criticism, throwing his simple childhood faith into doubt and alienating him from the orthodoxy of his superiors. Because of bitter opposition to his liberal views from the reactionary Catholic hierarchy Renan was unable to rise in the French universities. So, sponsored by Emperor Napoleon III, he was sent to conduct a survey of archaeological sites in the Middle East. While travelling in the Holy Land he began to write the work which would bring him international fame and lasting notoriety: *La Vie de Jésus*.

Upon his return, Renan did eventually obtain the chair of Hebrew and Semitic Languages at the University of Paris, but he was suspended a mere four days after delivering his inaugural lecture in which he outraged the devout by referring to the founder of the Christian faith as: 'an incomparable *man*, so great that, although everything ought to be judged from the perspective of positive science, I should not wish to contradict those who, struck by the exceptional character of his work, call a *god*.'

The publication of his narrative of the life of Jesus a few months later in 1863 wrecked further possibility of academic advancement. Before the year was out, however, more than sixty thousand copies had been sold. At the age of forty, Renan found himself one of the most celebrated men of letters in France and a champion of free-thinkers, whether he wanted to be or not.

What was it about this life-story which made it such a massive best-seller while bringing down upon the head of its writer condemnation reminiscent of the Inquisition? Though the book could never have been written without the prior work of the German Biblical analysts (such as David Strauss's *Leben Jesu*, translated into English by George Eliot) Renan's popularity was not based upon dry, abstracted textual exegesis. Rather he painted a romantic picture, a noble tragedy which would doubtless have succoured late nineteenth century apostates, no longer able to profess a faith which contradicted the laws of natural science but not yet ready to bid farewell to the old, old story and stare into the abyss of oblivion.

If Frazer infers a Jesus who must be just one of many dying gods – a prototype of Myth – Renan's Nazarene is a real creature of flesh and blood, of history, of psychology – a living man, but nevertheless 'the creator of the eternal religion of humanity'. Renan gave his readers a story of a possible Jesus to replace the theology of the church's impossible Christ and to rival the mythological dismissal of the nihilists. This is a biography stripped of all supernatural elements: the virgin birth, the exorcisms, the healings and raisings from the dead, even the resurrection – a Jesus for the times.

In the first chapter Renan asserts: 'As soon as man became distinguished from the animal, he became religious – that is to say, he saw something beyond the phenomena, and for himself something beyond death. This sentiment, during some thousands of years, became corrupted.' The ministry of Jesus was to purge natural religion of these corrupt excrescences; to establish 'a pure worship, a religion without priests and external observances, resting on the feelings of the heart'; to 'throw off the yoke of rites and ceremonies'; to found 'the pure worship of all ages, of all lands, which all elevated souls will practise until the end of time … and if other planets have inhabitants gifted with reason and morality, their religion cannot be different from that which Jesus proclaimed'; to preach the absolute gospel that 'the Kingdom of Heaven is within' – a Jesus as Renan would wish him to be.

Twenty three years after *The Life of Jesus* Renan moved from biography to drama, from the shores of the Galilean lake to another lake in the Alban Hills. His new central character might, however, be a transformation of the ideal protagonist of the old work which had brought its author such applause and such opprobrium. Antistius, the Priest of Nemi, might be another version of Renan's Jesus. He might also be a disguised embodiment of the dramatist himself.

Le Prêtre de Nemi

Perhaps Renan's visit to Nemi in 1881 provided the idea that 'one of those old fables of antiquity which have a deeper meaning than all our political treatises' might provide a fertile spring for a story which would allow him to present further reflections on the origin and evolution of the religious impulse, this time in dramatic form. His sources were the same classical writers Frazer knew so well:

> My subject is taken from stories about the temple of Diana on the shores of the lake of Nemi, the priesthood of which was

2) John Savile Lumley, 1st Baron Savile of Rufford (1818–1896) – Archaeologist of the Temple of Diana at Nemi.

3) James George Frazer (1854–1941) – Author of *The Golden Bough*.

4) Frazer's frontispiece to every edition of *The Golden Bough* – engraving from the original painting by J.M.W. Turner actually depicting Lake Avernus not Nemi!

5) Ernest Renan (1823–1892) – Author of *Le Prêtre de Nemi*.

legitimated by his having killed his predecessor in hand-to-hand combat. Strabo wrote: 'That meant he must constantly have his sword in hand, must be always on his guard, ready to repel any attack that might be made upon him.' Caligula, who was not devoid of wit, was the first to mock this unique custom. The *Rex Nemorensis* of his day was an old man whom the years had made respectable. Caligula, that street-kid, who through the accident of becoming Caesar held the destinies of the world, forced the old Priest to duel with a gladiator far stronger than himself, who became his successor.

(Preface to *Le Prêtre de Nemi* – my translation)

Renan called his *drames philosophiques* 'the recreations of an idealist,' plays written to be read and thought about rather than to be staged and experienced. He regarded drama as a form worthy of conveying complex philosophical ideas: 'Truths do not have to be directly affirmed nor directly denied; they should not have to be the object of demonstration. All we have to do is present them in their various facets, to show strength, weakness, necessity and how they are connected.' The lesson of Shakespeare is that drama can free the scholar from the tyranny of 'real history': 'It is not only events which have really happened that are of interest. Alongside real history is an ideal history, which never actually happened, but which, in an ideal sense, must have happened very many times. '*Coriolanus* and *Julius Caesar* are not accurate depictions of Roman custom, they are psychological studies.' Drama also gives the man of letters, whose own expressed opinions are continually subjected to critical judgment, freedom to put views antithetical to his own into the mouths of the fictional characters he creates: 'I am not a priest, I am an intellectual; and, as such, I have to see all sides.' This liberty, however, comes at a price for a writer who had become accustomed to being misinterpreted:

The essence of dialogue lies in putting different opinions into play, and the essence of drama is to put different characters into opposition. Thus writers are exposed to the strange misunderstandings of critics who select extracts hastily so the most contradictory views are attributed to us.

The setting of Renan's play is the 'long white town' of Alba Longa, leader of the alliance of the cities of Latium. The time is shortly before the mythical foundation in the seventh century BCE of Rome, whose buildings can be seen rising up on the Palatine Hill on the horizon. The presiding god of the region is Jupiter Latiaris and the spiritual and economic centrality of the city has traditionally been guaranteed by the goddess Diana. Her shrine by the Lake of Nemi is visited by supplicants from near and far who entreat her healing powers through sacrifices conducted by her dread Priest and pilgrims who seek the wisdom of her oracle, the Sibyl. Alba was once a strong kingdom but now is a liberal republic whose future is under threat. Though the Roman twins Romulus and Remus are said to be descended from the ancient kings of the Latin League, the city has twice been weakened through conflict with the upstart power.

In the Preface to his play Renan explicitly connects its subject with that of his most controversial work: 'I wanted to develop an idea comparable to Messianism among the Hebrews'. His aspiration is to show that 'faith will ultimately triumph through religious and moral progress, notwithstanding the continual victories of folly and evil … a good cause will gain ground in spite of the bitterness, the disgrace, the failure, even the errors of its apostles and martyrs.' But there is another stated purpose: 'I wanted to bring to light the iron rule that in politics crime is often rewarded and virtue as often punished.' So the sub-textual contexts of *Le Prêtre de Nemi* are not just religious but political. These themes reflect not only the personal experiences of the writer but also the historical times in which he was writing.

In 1869, as storm clouds gathered over the disputed territory of Alsace-Lorraine and French patriots began rattling rusty sabres,

Renan was reluctantly persuaded to leave his study and stand for election: 'A private life would be my happiness; but such a life appears to me tainted by selfishness.' A revolutionary in thought only, always suspicious of popular democracy and previously dependent on the patronage of the aristocratic elite, he became a candidate for the Liberal Opposition on a ticket of 'No War. No Revolution.' A platform of peace at any price was hardly going to win many votes – naturally he was defeated. The following year France disastrously declared war.

For someone who had been so influenced by philosophy and scholarship from across the border, the German hostilities were: 'a crime ... a fit of stark, staring madness!' Prussian militarism constituted 'the greatest heartache of my life.' As Madame Darmesteter (Mary Robinson) wrote in her memoir of Renan, published in 1897, five years after his death:

> France was doomed to defeat; and, in his prophetic vision, Renan wept her defeat in tears of blood, for she suffered it at the hands of his ideal. All his life he had dreamed of uniting France and Germany. Behold, the nation to which Renan owed all that was best in him – the nation of Goethe, Kant – revealed itself as a rout of drunken troopers! Exposed to the long agony of the siege [of Paris], unpopular, without credit in the eyes of the violent factions which divided the country, Renan continued to preach his message and to show the sacred hope of a future redeemed by the humiliations of the present.

Though it might be too crude to equate France with Latium and Germany with Rome, this biographer's conclusion was surely correct in equating Renan himself with his fictional Priest of Nemi: 'Let us then imagine him, like his own Antistius, a victim to the strife of the ideal with base reality.'

Renan wrote that his play is concerned with:

The selfishness of the nobility, the folly of the populace, the powerlessness of the intelligentsia, the villainy of deceitful religion, the weakness of a reforming priest, the easy deceptions of patriotism, the delusions of liberalism, the incurable wickedness of bad people.

His play is a product of war. But it is an equally pessimistic product of the religious controversies he had done so much to provoke:

> I have created a Priest of Nemi, in a remote age, who is an enlightened man who wishes to purify an absurd old creed and I have shown the consequences which follow from this tentative attempt to introduce a little reason into human affairs. These consequences are two-fold: firstly, the mob, which can only find assurance in the performance of the ancient rite, demands a villain for its priest; secondly, the reforming priest soon comes to realise that, despite the best intentions, he has done more harm than good, that he has damaged his country, which is founded upon widely accepted prejudices.

The reforming mission of the Priest Antistius is a failure. 'The result is a sad tableau.' In a later American biography of Renan in 1921 Lewis Freeman Mott summarised the story as follows:

> In place of the ancient assassin, the author has imagined an enlightened priest, who discards antiquated traditions and practices, and devotes himself to the amelioration of humanity, to the service of reason, and to the worship of the infinite. All are opposed to him except two lovers, who have open hearts, and Liberalis, head of the republic, who has an open mind; but the lovers are without influence and Liberalis is compelled to yield to the mob. Antistius has gained the Temple without slaying his predecessor, and the people demand for the office a vile murderer; he has abolished sacrifices, and the people demand the immolation of human victims; he has substituted reason, justice and real worship for out-worn superstitions,

corrupt practices and senseless rites, and the people demand the customs of their fathers. On his death, his murderer [Casca] succeeds him for a moment amid general rejoicing, and when he too falls, we are left to infer that his fellow brigand, Ladro, is to gain the appointment through subserviency to the leader of the aristocrats, though Ganeo, a despicable assistant to Antistius, who has lost all faith and virtue as a result of the too exalted teachings of his noble master, would be a fitter candidate for head of the Temple. This overthrow, together with an insane declaration of war by Alba Longa against Rome, constitutes the entire plot. In their acts of folly the populace, led by a demagogue [Cethegus], a fanatic [Dolabella] and a self-seeking nobleman [Methius], force their chief, Liberalis, to proceed against his better judgment.

This deft précis omits mention of one aspect of Renan's drama which seems troublingly anachronistic to the modern reader. Neither the classical sources nor the archaeological record confirm the presence of a female oracle at the temple. Yet in the play the young Sibyl, Carmenta, plays an important role: firstly in her subordinate relationship to the Priest she serves and worships; then in her satisfying revenge of his murder; and finally in her soothsaying prediction of a future faith, which will come from the East to supplant the old polytheism of false gods with a new monotheism of One God.

In *La Vie de Jésus* Renan had written: 'The conviction (of women) that God is in them, and occupies himself perpetually with them, is so strong that they have no fear of obtruding themselves upon others'. In the Preface to *Le Prêtre de Nemi* he perpetuated this misogynistic strain: 'Woman, with the simplicity of her faith, her lack of knowledge, her naivety ... sees what is essential better than men. No mother needs a system of moral philosophy in order to love her child. No well-brought up young woman needs a theory to preserve her chastity.'

The only other female character in the play is Dolabella, a superstitious fanatic who puts her faith in ritual action, the answer to her people's problems will lie in a reversion to their age-old rituals whilst further protecting themselves by the importation of even more foreign idols. Carmenta puts into practice her belief that religion must be revived through self-sacrificing purity. Where do these patriarchal ideas come from?

Although Renan explicitly distanced himself from the positivism of Auguste Comte, which he found 'honourable' but 'analytical, dry, negative, incapable of understanding the things of the heart and the imagination', nevertheless the so-called 'founder of sociology' cast a long shadow, not least in such essentialist notions of a masculine tendency towards the intellectual and rational, contrasting with and complementing a feminine predisposition towards the emotional and the altruistic.

In Renan's Alba Longa, as in his Palestine, it is 'Woman' who seems to carry the torch for the natural transcendent impulse which will redeem our fallen species.

Frazer and Renan

Unlike his friend's dismissive opinion of Renan's scholarship, Frazer's estimation could not be higher – though it wasn't publicly expressed until nearly thirty years after Robertson Smith's death. In an address delivered in French to the Ernest Renan Society in December 1920 Frazer declared to the Parisian audience: 'I dare even say that among your great writers there is none with whom I feel such a close and deep sympathy as Renan' (my translation). In this uncharacteristically succinct and personal speech, together with the preface written to accompany its subsequent publication, Frazer distilled the similarities of their sensibilities and their approaches to the study of religion.

He found so much in common, not least their mutual heritage: 'As a Breton Renan was of the old Celtic blood which runs in my own Scots veins' and this made them both 'dreamers, romantics' rather than 'pure rationalists.' Both were sceptics: 'scepticism is always right, dogmatism is always wrong; because what humans consider truths today will become the falsehoods of tomorrow.' Both were, like most free-thinkers of the age, true 'progressivists'. And here again, an unacknowledged echo of positivist philosophy might perhaps be detected.

Comte had proposed a 'Law of Three Stages' in which mankind evolved through three succeeding evolutionary levels: the Theological (which itself evolved from Fetishism, to Polytheism before developing into Monotheism); followed by the Metaphysical, before eventually arriving at a state of Science. Renan had declared in his early work *The Future of Science* (written in 1849 but not published until 1890): 'This is a formula containing a great part of the truth', but he found Comte's thought severely limited: 'Poetry, religion, imagination, all these are ignored.' Nevertheless, in *Le Prêtre de Nemi* Renan constructed a narrative of human thought which was, in many ways, remarkably similar. Our species, it would seem, has a natural tendency towards transcendence; this original impulse becomes overlaid with the superstition of miraculous fable and ridiculous ritual; in time the spirit of mankind will overthrow the false gods and polytheism will give way to monotheism. This is, however, merely another transitory stage on the ultimate journey to a higher ideal – what Renan's Antistius called Divinity and which we, like Renan's Jesus, will find within ourselves.

Frazer too, hardly coincidentally, postulated his own 'Law of Three' – an equally speculative evolutionary schema of the advance of the human mind. From an age of Magic, in which primitive philosophers unsuccessfully sought to influence the forces of nature through imitative actions, mankind came to the sad realisation that sticking pins in wax effigies or chanting spells over nail-clippings had no palpable effect; therefore our forebears came up with the idea of Religion, when priests sought to gain predictable favours for their people through the propitiation of super-human beings more powerful than ourselves; but now a new age of Science is in the ascendant and previously misguided attempts to control and order the universe will at last be founded on rationality. Mind you, Frazer ascertained, those primordial magicians were on the right track all along, only their empirical knowledge was deficient – it was those supernaturalists who were definitely wrong. The fatal web of humanity is 'woven of three different threads: the black thread of magic, the red thread of religion, and the white thread of science.'

However different in nuance these formulations might be, they all end up with the triumph of Science, an inevitable advance which places modern western 'civilization' at the apex of social and mental evolution. Hardly surprising these nineteenth century notions have been subjected to twentieth century ridicule and contempt. But it would be entirely unfair to accuse either Frazer or Renan of espousing the kind of fundamentalist scientific optimism all too prevalent in the twenty-first century. Both had a profound appreciation of what would be lost in this uneven progression. Both were at heart deeply melancholic. Both had to struggle to reconcile their stated trust in a possible rational future with their experiential knowledge of an all too illogical present and a nostalgia for what they saw as, in spite of themselves, a far less troubled past.

In *Psyche's Task* (the title referring to a quotation from Milton about the incessant labour of Psyche to separate the seeds of good from the seeds of evil) Frazer wrote:

> Man is a very curious animal, and the more we know of his habits the more curious does he appear. He may be the most rational of the beasts, but certainly he is the most absurd. Even the saturnine wit of Swift, unaided by a knowledge of savages, fell far short of the reality in his attempt to set human folly in a strong light. Yet the odd thing is that in spite, or perhaps

by virtue, of his absurdities man moves steadily upwards; the more we learn of his past history the more groundless does the old theory of his degeneracy prove to be. From false premises he often arrives at sound conclusions: from a chimerical theory he deduces a salutary practice.

How similar are the sentiments expressed in this passage of Renan's (from an uncited source which forms the epigraph to William Barry's biography of 1905):

> An immense river of oblivion sweeps us onward into a gulf without a name. O abyss, thou art the only God! The tears of all peoples are tears indeed; the dreams of all wise men have in them a parcel of the truth. All here below is but symbol and dream. The gods pass away like men; it would not be well did they last forever. The faith which we have held ought never to be a chain. We have done our duty by it when we have carefully wrapped it round in the purple shroud wherein the dead gods sleep.
>
> My life has been such as I desired, such as I conceived to be the best. Had I to live it over again, I should make very little change. On the other hand, I am not much afraid of the future. I shall have my biography and my legend.

In Frazer's address to the Renan Society, given only a few years after the ending of the First World War and the beginning of the Bolshevik revolution, he attempts to bridge the gulf between the ideal of progress and the reality of human folly: 'Civilization is standing once again in the west of Europe but has been overturned by an eruption of savagery in the east… Beneath the surface of the civilized world a deep layer of savagery lives on, a savagery not yet dead, but alive and lively, ever ready to boil up and crack the thin, brittle skin of the civilization which would suppress it.' Small wonder he found a fellow-feeling in *Le Prêtre de Nemi*.

Ironically, it was this very nightmare of Savage Survival always prone to erupt from within the mind of civilized man, which struck the deepest chord, to be embraced rather than stifled by those modernist writers whom Frazer influenced so profoundly, surely contrary to his avowed intentions.

Did the conventional Renan welcome the triumph of doubt which his work inaugurated? Did the conservative Frazer regret the psychic whirlwind of unconscious emotion which his work unleashed?

Farewell to Nemi

The celebrated Scot at last made explicit homage to his French counterpart when talking to his compatriot disciples. It was not, however, the play which he credited with inspiration. Rather it was Renan's metaphor of the bells of Rome forever tolling through the ruins of the Eternal City which Frazer admitted he had borrowed for his final paragraph. But he was too honest not to confess: 'Unfortunately a friend who is very learned and somewhat meticulous pointed out to me that, in fact, at Nemi one cannot hear the bells of Rome as they are too far away. This truth is indisputable, so, with regret, in the final edition of my book I replaced the bells of Rome with the bells of Aricia.'

And so *The Golden Bough* comes to its conclusion:

> The place has changed but little since Diana received the homage of her worshippers in the sacred grove. The temple of the sylvan goddess, indeed, has vanished and the King of the Wood no longer stands sentinel over the Golden Bough. But Nemi's woods are still green, and as the sunset fades above them in the west, there comes to us, borne on the swell of the wind, the sound of the church bells of Aricia ringing the Angelus.

This apparently regrettable substitution proves to be entirely fortuitous for the comparative method. The Ariccian chimes ring out from the dome of Bernini's baroque basilica dedicated to the Assumption of the Blessed Virgin Mary. Her feast day in mid-August falls at exactly the same time of the year as the festival when once the goddess Diana was worshipped by those slaves for whom she was the divine patroness:

> Sweet and solemn they chime out from the distant town and die lingeringly away across the wide Campagnan marshes. *Le roi est morte, vive le roi! Ave Maria!*

Pilgrimage to Nemi

I finally arrived at Renan's neglected play on a long route via a childhood fascination with the votive objects exhibited in a local museum, passing through an adolescent exposure to the wonders of the world in *The Golden Bough*, culminating in a recent unexpected pilgrimage to the site of Diana's temple. Throughout this life-long journey the compulsive attraction of 'the priest who slew the slayer and shall himself be slain' remained unabated. This mythological character is a chilling figure in whatever artistic guise he might appear: whether encountered in the dead youthful hero reincarnated as the bearded devotee of Kuntze's fading wall paintings; in the doomed progressive reformer of Renan's drama; in the stern and sinister escaped slave of Frazer's opening chapter; or, most especially, in Nottingham's double-headed herm of the old occupant and the young claimant.

Though the historians of classical art might refuse to accept the bust as a depiction of the *Rex Nemorensis*, Two-Face remains by far the most evocative embodiment of the 'ghastly priest' in either of his forms: agèd occupant or youthful adversary. But I claim the right to project onto these staring eyes a completely different set of psychological emotions from those which has been heretofore read into their stony visages. Whatever these faces may have originally represented, for me they depict an uneasy coexistence of the Past and the Future.

Is the old man really 'haggard and scared'? His eyes may be 'wild' but they seem far from 'anxious'; the cracked grin on his bearded face rather shows that he's had a good life but won't be sorry to let it go. His grim smile offers a sardonic reproach to the aspiration of some young Johnny-come-lately with the nerve to take the place of one who knows only too well what trials his successor will have to undergo, who understands all too clearly that a determined pursuit can never be fulfilled except by death. The young man is clearly more virile, his cold gaze might indeed be 'steadfast', but it is surely far from secure. In a gladiatorial contest the young pretender would definitely win, but he seems anxious lest the prize might not be worth the endeavour.

Perhaps it's happier looking backwards. Perhaps the past, for all its superstitious folly, holds more consolation. Perhaps the future, for all its scientific rationality, promises little else but doubt and uncertainty.

Could this be why the story, in all its many variants and reinterpretations, remains so resonant? Could it be that this violent tale somehow represents the existential quest of all of us? To seek out and pluck the sacred bough in the dark, wild wood of the imagination – that liminal zone of danger but also of exhilaration where normal rules no longer apply. To triumph, bruised and wounded from the pursuit and, undefeated, tell of the visions granted on the journey. But might we not also share the dread of the *Rex Nemorensis*, fearful that a dark figure waits somewhere in the shadows, biding time before delivering the inevitable mortal blow. And might we not harbour a lurking suspicion that this armed slayer, this escaped slave, will, when he does eventually appear, be no stranger… because he comes from deep within our very selves.

The Priest of Nemi will never die. The King of the Wood will forever be reborn.

The Translation of *Le Prêtre de Nemi*

Though this translation is by no means literal linguistically it is completely faithful philosophically. Renan may have expected his *drame philosophe* to be played at the Comédie Française or, failing that aspiration, on the stage of some Parisian boulevard theatre, because he gives the instruction: 'To avoid any suggestion of local colour the cast should be dressed as the characters in Masaccio's paintings in Santa Maria del Carmine in Florence or like the Romans as depicted by Mantegna in the Church of the Eremitani in Padua.' As it turned out his oeuvre has never, to the best of my knowledge, been through the refiner's fire of audience reception. This version has, however, been produced for performance. So I have introduced an entirely new Prologue for purposes of exposition and have also substituted stage directions with the voice of a Narrator.

Renan adopted the now out-moded convention of numbering scenes whenever a new character appears on stage. I have taken a more fluid approach with scenes only ending whenever there is a change in either time or place and no act breaks. Therefore scene and act numbers in the French version do not correspond to the scenes in this translation.

Though the political and theological positions of Renan's characters are always clear, their voices are rarely individuated. So I have, to a certain extent, given the main characters idiomatic speech patterns without, I hope, betraying the original. I have also tried to simplify and clarify the voices of Renan's choruses of the various factions of Alba Longa.

This translation was aided by a Grant For The Arts from the Arts Council of England, for which I am most grateful. It is to be given a public reading at Nottingham Playhouse to coincide with a major exhibition of the Nemi Collection at Nottingham Castle in 2013. Perhaps then it will become clear whether the play deserves a full-scale production or whether it should remain as an undoubtedly significant contribution to the history of ideas rather than to the history of the theatre.

FURTHER READING

The Nottingham Collection:

Mysteries of Diana: The Antiquities from Nemi in Nottingham, ed. A. G. MacCormick (Nottingham: Castle Museum, 1983)

James Frazer:

The Golden Bough: A Study in Religion and Magic, third edition (London: Macmillan, 1906-1915), 12 vols. Abridged edition, 1922
Aftermath: A Supplement to The Golden Bough (London: Macmillan, 1936)
Psyche's Task : A Discourse Concerning The Influence of Superstition On The Growth of Institutions (London: Macmillan, 1909)
Address to the Ernest Renan Society 1920, reprinted in *Garnered Sheaves* (London, Macmillan 1931)
Robert Ackermann, *J.G. Frazer: His Life and Work* (Cambridge: Cambridge University Press 1987)
Robert Fraser, *The Making of The Golden Bough: The Origins and Growth of an Argument* (London, Macmillan, 1990)

Edmund Leach:

'Golden Bough or Gilded Twig', *Daedalus*, vol 90, no 2 (Spring 1961), 371–99
'On the Founding Fathers: Fraser and Malinowski', *Encounter*, 25 (1965), 24–36
'Frazer Reconsidered', *Guardian*, 30 July 1970
'Reflections On A Visit To Nemi: Did Frazer Get It Wrong?' *Anthropology Today*, 1 (April 1985), 2–3.

Ernest Renan:

La Vie de Jésus 1863 (First English Translation 1864)
Le Prêtre de Nemi 1886
The Future of Science written 1849, published 1890 (First English Translation 1891)

Madame James Darmesteter (Mary Robinson), *The Life of Ernest Renan* (London: Methuen, 1897)
Francis Espinasse, *Life of Ernest Renan* (London: Walter Scott Ltd, 1897)
William Barry, *Ernest Renan* (New York: Scribner, 1905)
Lewis Freeman Mott, *Ernest Renan* (New York: D. Appleton 1921)

William Roberston Smith, Review of *Histoire du Peuple d'Israël*, *Historical Review*, vol 2, no 6 (January 1888), 303–17

LIST OF ILLUSTRATIONS

1) Great Is Diana – statue of the goddess in the Ny Carlsberg Glyptotek, Copenhagen [p. v]

2) John Savile Lumley, 1st Baron Savile of Rufford (1818–1896) – Archaeologist of the Temple of Diana at Nemi [p. xix]

3) James George Frazer (1854–1941) – Author of *The Golden Bough* [p. xix]

4) Frazer's frontispiece to every edition of *The Golden Bough* – engraving from the original painting by J.M.W. Turner actually depicting Lake Avernus not Nemi! [p. xxx]

5) Ernest Renan (1823–1892) – Author of *Le Prêtre de Nemi* [p. xxx]

6), 7) and 8) Savile's documentation of his excavation at Nemi – originals in Nottingham Castle [p. xxxxvii]

9) and 10) The Temple site today [p. xxxxviii]

11), 12) and 13) The Nottingham Double-Headed Herm – 'Aquatic Monsters' or the Old Priest and his Usurper? [p. il]

14), 15) and 16) The Copenhagen Double-Headed Herm – personifications of Lake Albano and Lake Nemi? [p. l]

17), 18) and 19) The Nemi Double-Headed Herm – Hippolytus and Virbius? [p. li]

20) The Temptation of Hippolytus by Phaedre [p. lii]

21) Diana's Sacred Grove [p. lii]

22) The Resurrection of Hippolytus by Asclepius [p. liii]

23) The Priest of Nemi sacrifices to Diana [p. liv]

The murals in plates 20–24 are by Taddeo Kuntze in the Museo del Grand Tour, Locanda Martorelli, Ariccia, Italy.

6)

7)

8)

9)

10)

14)

15)

16)

17)

18)

19)

li

20)

21)

lii

22)

23)

THE PRIEST OF NEMI

DRAMATIS PERSONAE

IN THE CITY:

TITIUS
VOLTINIUS } Citizens of Alba.
TERTIUS
METIUS Leader of the Patricians.
LIBERALIS Spokesman of the Democratic Faction.
CETHEGUS Demagogic Rabble-Rouser.
DOLABELLA Religious Fanatic.
HERDONIUS Aged Messenger.
SERVANT At the House of Metius.
CASCA & LATRO Assassins.

CITIZENS OF ALBA LONGA
COMMONERS
BOURGEOISIE
FOLLOWERS OF THE DEMAGOGUE
PEASANTS

AT THE TEMPLE:

ANTISTIUS: Priest of Nemi.
CARMENTA: Sybil of the Temple of Diana.
SACRIFICULUS & GANEO: Servers at the Temple and the Cave of the Sybil.

CONSULTANTS OF THE ORACLE:

LEADER OF THE HERNICIAN DELEGATION
HERNICIAN PRISONERS
MATERNA
VIRGINUS
VIRGINIA
DEPUTATION OF THE AEQUICOLAE

PORCIA
LEPORINUS

A PROPHET OF ISRAEL

This play demands a certain knowledge of the geographical, historical and theological background of a story which is set in pre-classical times before the foundation of the city of Rome. So a Prologue has been added to supply some context for a modern reader and has been given to the character of HERDONIUS *who plays an expositionary role throughout the drama. Subsequently, stage directions have also been given to a* NARRATOR *for purposes of performance.*

PROLOGUE.

HERDONIUS: Hearken to old Herdonius, agèd citizen of Alba Longa, fairest and most venerable of all the cities of Latium, foundation and head of power, temporal and spiritual, for the Latin tribes confederated against our enemies in defence of our culture and our language. Well... there was a time when I might have spoken such words in all pride and truthfulness. These days I can no longer have such confidence.

For those distant scions of our ancient king Latinus, the twin brothers Romulus and Remus, have broken away from their fatherland and set up state, over there to the north east, where Roma Quadrata rises up on the Palatine Hill. In the past ten years these Romans, as they're calling themselves, have twice bested our armies and demoralised our nation. Now, if the oracles are to be believed, these defeats might only be the beginning of our misfortunes.

From ancient times the fortune of Alba Longa and our allies has been protected and vouchsafed by the goddess we worship at her temple in the sacred grove on the shores of the Lake Nemi – which we call Diana's Mirror. Our Lady is a chaste deity of many parts: she is the goddess of the moon, of the hunt, of woodlands, of wild creatures as well as domestic animals. Barren wives and women in labour are her special worshippers, because she presides over fertility and childbirth. But, for those who beseech her in the proper manner, Diana might be entreated to cure every sort of sickness.

Ever since the good old days supplicants have come here from far and wide to petition her assistance; to make whatever sacrifices they could afford; to purchase votive offerings of precious metal, of costly marble, of humble clay and, from the poor who could come up with money for nothing better, even of bread – which at least kept our bakers busy. Her devotees have heard and obeyed the words of the soothsayer, the Sibyl, speaking through mortal female mouth from her hallowed cave the divine ordinances of the goddess who communes with us here below from her moonlit realm above.

This city has thrived from the desperate requests of these unfortunate pilgrims. You can be sure that not only the Priest of Nemi but each of the Servers at the shrine of the goddess always got a decent cut.

Ever since I was a child I was taught that our temple at Nemi was special, different from any other holy place in Latium. Because in this sanctuary the priest had to be an escaped slave who has run away like a deer in the hunt. One sacrosanct commandment prevailed: a new candidate could acquire the post of priest at any time, provided he could find the Golden Bough in the sacred grove, hunt down the present incumbent and challenge him to a duel… a gladiatorial fight to the death.

Should this criminal newcomer be successful and murder the old priest then he would reign in his place as *Rex Nemorensis*: King of the Wood. A fine old custom!

Why is everything going so badly for us now? Why has the goddess turned her stern face against those who have always reverenced her? Could it be that our new minister, Antistius, has abandoned the ancient rituals of the temple and is attempting to impose a new religion? Could it be that the Priest of Nemi is no proper priest?

SCENE ONE.

> NARRATOR: *As the sun sets over the sea towards Ostia Tiberina in the west the* CITIZENS *take in the cool air on the walls of Alba Longa, a large terrace overlooking the great green oak trees of the sacred grove on the slope of the volcanic rock which towers over the lake of Nemi.* TITIUS *and* VOLTINIUS *look eastwards to the horizon.*

TITIUS: Who would ever have thought that the downfall of Latium is destined to come from that damned hillock? And perhaps even one day the whole world too will tremble before Rome… if we're to believe the oracles of the Sibyl.

VOLTINIUS: Take no notice of Carmenta's wild fantasies. One thing is certain: these Roman upstarts are a strange combination of law-givers and law-breakers. Every day their victory gets closer. No longer satisfied with vanquishing us here in Alba…

TITIUS: Which is, after all, where their ancestors hail from in the first place…

VOLTINIUS: …these Romans are aiming to run this new city of theirs as if the rest of us will simply fall in line with their conviction that whatever they do will be for the greater good of all mankind. From those seven little heaps of nothing they act as if it's their absolute right to impose a new world order. Look at that temple they're raising up on the side of the Palatine Hill! To Jupiter! Our god! The fateful echoes of prophecy decree that this temple will stand at epicentre of the world to come.

TITIUS: Yet more oracles! I've long since ceased believing in any of them. Mind you, that's of scant consequence, seeing as how the rest of the world seems to put so much trust in sooth-saying. What I can't understand, though, is why these brigands, who put themselves beyond the pale of all law human and divine, don't leave us alone and turn upon each other.

VOLTINIUS: Ah, well, that's politics. Discord is the sign of life and strength. The very ones who are so keen to preserve law and order today were once all anarchists. Every conservative has an outlaw for an ancestor. Look at what happened to Hercules after he stole the oxen of Cacus – he became the staunchest defender of private property.

TITIUS: It's hard to be vanquished by parvenus.

VOLTINIUS: True enough. But for us right now revenge is impossible, defeat is inevitable. We may be far more advanced, more civilised, than our enemies; we're certainly their social superiors. But what they have is force. The more barbaric we consider them the more certain they are to conquer us. A state such as ours, torn apart internally with the disease of progress, is useless at warfare. We're like a man with a deep scar on his leg. Ordinarily the wound would cause no problems. But, should he ever have to make some violent effort, then the scar opens up and his Achilles heel is revealed. There's no greater test of the character of a nation than war. But the game's not equal between ourselves and Rome. We are risking our all. Should Alba be vanquished one more time, it'll be the end of us, we will cease to exist. It's not the same for Rome. We face an opponent who has little to lose, who is not staking everything. Nevertheless... the wheel of fortune spins slowly and there's nothing we can do to speed its turning. We have to learn patience. If we can play the long game we might win out one day.

TITIUS: In the long run we'll all be dead. Your argument doesn't take into account that people are creatures of passion who act from instinct. We have an enemy within who are on the side of these robbers. They're sending out signals from inside our walls to the Palatine Hill.

VOLTINIUS: What are you talking about?

TITIUS: The oracles from the Sibyl.

VOLTINIUS: Carmenta?

TITIUS: Of course. Hasn't she proclaimed that the destiny of Latium will ultimately be accomplished by Rome? What else would you call that but treachery? And what about her master: Antistius, Priest of Nemi? His uncalled-for innovations are undermining the very foundations of our ramparts.

VOLTINIUS: Well, yes. We should be worried when priests start preaching reformation.

TITIUS: They never know when to stop.

VOLTINIUS: Mind you – and between ourselves – isn't Antistius only saying what you and I are thinking?

TITIUS: He is?

VOLTINIUS: You can attach too much importance to religion. The common folk don't put quite so much confidence in faith as you might imagine.

No, it's that demagogue Cethagus and his rabble who are far more dangerous. Class war will be the end of civilised society. The plebs believe a city is made up of their houses. They have no idea that a city is only as strong as the ramparts. These walls are the defence of all our institutions. The commoners want democracy. But without noble families and time-honoured institutions our city is wide open. It's the patricians who defend society, so they have every right to their privileges. Without the aristocrats nothing would exist.

TITIUS: True enough perhaps... when society is under threat.

VOLTINIUS: When is society not under threat? Every society has enemies... except for the fabled isles of the Hesperides – which I suspect don't exist anywhere on this earth. Life is a constant struggle against the causes of destruction. Whoever does not defend himself is lost.

NARRATOR: *Groups of* CITIZENS *are forming on the ramparts.*

FIRST CITIZEN: The most dangerous animal is a hungry animal. When someone with an empty belly comes begging for work it's best to give him a job to take his mind off his misery.

SECOND CITIZEN: But our resources are not endless. Our forefathers, at great cost to themselves, dug out the channel for the lake of Nemi. They didn't know why.

THIRD CITIZEN: An oracle told them.

SECOND CITIZEN: So what should we do now?

FIRST CITIZEN: We opened another watercourse on the north side last year... we could always fill it up again.

THIRD CITIZEN: But we need that channel.

FIRST CITIZEN: That proves my point. Fill that ditch in now

and then we can dig a new one next year.

NARRATOR: *Some of the* COMMON PEOPLE *congregate around* DOLABELLA, *a religious fanatic.*

FIRST COMMONER: Terrible times!

SECOND COMMONER: Nothing but pain and misery.

FIRST COMMONER: Terrifying prodigies!

SECOND COMMONER: The harvest will be lost this year.

FIRST COMMONER: Plague threatens us. Tell us why, Dolabella!

DOLABELLA: The reason is simple. Diana no longer has a true priest. The goddess exacts her vengeance. Diana's temple is the navel of the world; the order of the universe depends upon the proper observance of the rites at her shrine. The gods are just like us… it's all a case of give and take. When Jupiter Latiaris was satisfied with the sacrificial victims we provided for him he looked after us here in Latium. When Diana was sanctified by the priest she loved she granted us protection. Nowadays the old ways are being chopped and changed. This so-called priest who presides over the sacred grotto today is devoid of solemnity. Antistius neglects the proper traditions. He didn't even kill his predecessor with his own bare hands as the good old custom demands.

FIRST COMMONER: He doesn't even look like a priest. Everyone should play his proper role. The duty of a priest is to preside over the time-honoured ceremonies, laid down before he came along.

NARRATOR: *The agèd HERDONIUS comes forward to give his opinion:*

HERDONIUS: Listen to me: old Herdonius! I was around long before any of you were even thought of. One thing is certain: what's going on round here right now is nothing like how it used to be in days gone by.

I saw some of those old priests. As human beings they might have been total bastards… but at least they always performed the proper rites so the people received the blessings of the goddess. I tell you, when I was a child I was taught that the temple was a sanctuary which harboured one criminal at a time. There weren't half some strange occupants. And there weren't many who lasted long. You remember the rule? Any new candidate could hunt down the old priest. But he wouldn't go willingly. The poor old priest could never sleep easy, never lower his guard. He had no idea who might have an eye on the office. He never had time to think, he was too busy worrying about his own survival.

FIRST COMMONER: That's what we expect. A priest isn't there to think.

SECOND COMMONER: Maybe so. But isn't it peculiar that such a barbaric custom should have become so respectable?

FIRST COMMONER: Time and tradition make all things respectable. That, my friend, is the human comedy in a nutshell. A wise man should go along with things as they are.

SECOND COMMONER: Antistius is the first of our priests who has refused to play to the crowd.

TITIUS: Such a man who sets his face against custom, who

maintains that use has become abuse, will always become a victim, whether he's right or wrong.

SECOND COMMONER: It'll end in tears.

HERDONIUS: Antistius deserves whatever's coming to him. Why should he want to mess about with ceremonies best left as they stand? This is what makes who we are.

NARRATOR: *The Aristocrat* METIUS *enters with the Democrat* LIBERALIS.

METIUS: We have suffered affronts from a would-be conqueror for ten years and if we put up with this outrage any longer we'll be finished as a people. The insult is compounded coming as it does from this new-fangled nation without history and which, moreover, owes everything to us. These Romans are a bunch of bandits, outlaws, refugees from who knows where. They are sullying the ancient glory of Alba Longa. Each day we sink deeper into the mire. And yet there are still Alban hearts which refuse to stand against them. We are riven with class division because we fail to unite and fight against the common foe. Hatred of Rome should be the defining mark of every true citizen of Alba. That cursed little township wants to overturn everything our great city stands for. I hate Rome. I hate these thankless, upstart johnny-come-latelys. That temple they're building on the Capitol to our great sky god Jupiter should instead be dedicated to Fortuna: goddess of thieves.

LIBERALIS: So you wish to go against the decrees of destiny, do you Metius? I suppose you want to bring back from the Hernicians the last descendent of our old kings: decent, simple Priscus?

METIUS: That might not be a bad idea, Liberalis. Priscus alone can claim incontestable possession of legitimate descent from the primordial sovereigns of Alba. Perhaps it is he who holds the title for our future restoration.

LIBERALIS: And I suppose you'd also restore the ancient laws of King Latinus?

METIUS: Why not? That would be best of all.

LIBERALIS: Won't you ever admit that human society has to progress? Can't you see there might even be some good in these Romans you label 'bandits'? You know they've made it their mission to abolish human sacrifice. What's wrong with that?

METIUS: So even you, Liberalis, are attracted by the follies of Antistius! A politician should never interfere with religion, that's all there is to it. Remove any one of these age-old practices and you'll destroy the whole. Try to bring rationality into religion and you'll end up an atheist. The first duty of a healthy state would be to exile Antistius… or kill him.

LIBERALIS: What could you possibly have against such a decent fellow? He's the first sane priest we've ever had. Because of his reformations that terrible sanctuary on the lake has been purged of its horrors. Antistius has abolished the hideous rite of succession by mortal combat. Was ever a custom more barbaric? In the name of the gods we are entreated to do good, yet we have honoured them by doing evil. Antistius has founded his holy orders on a purer source: the election of the people.

DOLABELLA: Listen to you! What can the popular mandate have to do with religion? The people should have no say over sacred laws. At this time there is effectively no priest of Nemi.

LIBERALIS: So much the better, if our priest should be in essence little more than a ruthless criminal.

METIUS: The rule of succession at the temple is a time-honoured rite, no stranger than any other religious observance. These mysteries go down so deep no human brain can ever penetrate their roots; they rise so high no human eye can ever see their summit. Our traditions are founded on obscure, impenetrable words from the oracle… so absurd yet at once so divine. These primeval enigmas possess a profound wisdom, whether our minds understand them or not. All I know is that to perform the rituals is to sanctify order. Order can only be maintained, in the divine sphere as well as in the worldly realm, by obeying clearly defined rules. The least doubt will shake the foundations. Doubt is evil. You democrats believe leadership should be won by election.

LIBERALIS: Axiomatically.

METIUS: How should such an election be decided?

LIBERALIS: On the basis of personal merit.

METIUS: And who is to determine who should have that claim? Only those of us who've been in this business have the experience to say who has the right to rule.

LIBERALIS: I put my trust in the popular vote.

METIUS: The popular vote! Even drawing lots is better than that. What is the outcome of democracy?

LIBERALIS: The will of the people.

METIUS: Not at all! Fraud, animosity, civil war. On the other hand, killing the previous occupant you seek to replace… well, at least that's straightforward, easy enough to prove. It gets rid of any argument and entirely accords with universal laws. In this world the sum total of happiness is limited. Those who set out to get what they want have to get rid of anyone who stands in their way. The winner must always do away with the person he wants to succeed. What could be better than a man with ambition finding himself face to face with some form of justice? And justice demands that he must one day be treated in exactly the same way he once treated another. After all, no-one is forced to take up such a perilous challenge. No-one who got what he wanted through violence could possibly object when violence is used against him. Such a man will be overthrown by the very same force he used to overthrow the one who came before him. Such chaos confirms the peculiar balance which governs the destiny of the cosmos.

LIBERALIS: Don't you think we ought to feel any gratitude to this man who has been inspired to do good, to turn his back on a violent law handed down from a barbarous past, a fatal legacy of a primitive age?

NARRATOR: *Agèd HERDONIUS has over-heard their argument.*

HERDONIUS: Listen to me! I was there when Antistius put an end to the tradition of blood and horror. When the old priest Tetricus realised that young Antistius desired reform he was so amazed he offered himself up as a human sacrifice to Jupiter Latiaris. Antistius took up his sword… We thought it was to strike the mortal blow… but it was to prevent Tetricus from killing himself! Was he right? Who knows? Antistius is certainly no coward. He fought off every one bringing sacrificial victims to the altar. He took over the temple by force all on his own and he put his weapon to the throat of

Tetricus. I was there. I saw it. All he had to do was thrust his blade into the old priest's jugular, two fingers deep, and he would have become the legitimate heir to the priesthood. But he wouldn't do it. I heard him say: 'Tetricus, I'm going to let you live, you despicable old priest. I'm sparing you so you can watch me put an end to this bloody ritual of yours.' Tetricus died a few days later anyway… of apoplectic rage! Then the populace put Antistius in his place… by election!

SECOND COMMONER: What an honourable man!

FIRST COMMONER: His actions won't do him any good. He should have done the decent thing and slain his predecessor. Nothing can go against fate according to the given laws.

THIRD COMMONER: We guide ourselves by obeying what has been laid down to the letter. That's the pole star of our faith.

FIRST COMMONER: What Antistius might think is right means nothing to us. We demand an outward and visible sign.

SECOND COMMONER: You may be right. Antistius is a fine man but everything's gone wrong for us since he took over the priesthood of Nemi.

THIRD COMMONER: There's never been a priest like him before.

FIRST COMMONER: He's a dreamer. Have you seen his eyes upturned towards the heavens?

SECOND COMMONER: He does look as if his prayers come from the heart.

THIRD COMMONER: The gods are deaf to the heart. They only listen to those words they've decreed should come from the lips.

FIRST COMMONER: And the actions they demand their priests to perform.

THIRD COMMONER: You have to wonder: Does Antistius take the gods seriously?

FIRST COMMONER: That's the very question: Does he really believe in anything?

THIRD COMMONER: You know Sacrificulus – one of the servers in the temple – he told me Antistius makes him repeat his prayers. Sacrificulus reckons the priest's trying to convert him to his beliefs.

SECOND COMMONER: It's the end of the world!

METIUS: Now do you understand what I've been saying, Liberalis? These plebeians know the duty of the priest: to trot out tried and tested catechisms – litanies which come out of the mouth, not from the heart. Antistius claims he wants to harness religion for the benefit of human progress, for the happiness of mankind, so that the world will be more rational, more just... and other such ridiculous absurdities. Religion exists to render to the gods what is their due. Which is exactly what the State also demands.

FIRST COMMONER: The patriarch Metius is right!

SECOND COMMONER: It's not for us to look too deeply into religion.

FIRST COMMONER: If we start questioning our rituals closely

we might end up finding they have no meaning.

SECOND COMMONER: I'm all for giving the gods their due, but you have to keep it in proportion. I've got nothing against religion, provided it's kept within limits.

THIRD COMMONER: All credit to the gods, but only religious maniacs believe they have total control.

SECOND COMMONER: Me, I'm a moderate. I'll have no truck with extremists.

FIRST COMMONER: What we want is a priest who stands before the altar, delivers the conventional words, acts out the obligatory gestures, and performs the necessary rituals.

THIRD COMMONER: Here comes Sacrificulus from the temple.

NARRATOR: *There is amazement all around as* SACRIFICULUS *enters, looking alarmed and sounding solemn.*

SACRIFICULUS: Another oracle from the Sibyl!

FIRST CITIZEN: Tell us what Carmenta said, Sacrificulus! Tell us now!

SACRIFICULUS: She has prophesied: 'Because of Rome, the language of Latium will become the language of the world.'

FIRST CITIZEN: The same old song! Rome, always Rome! She should get out of here and go and live in Rome.

VOLTINIUS: She's out of her mind. I always said the poor girl should have married young and led a normal life.

SECOND CITIZEN: This latest oracle of hers is a complete farce. Only three leagues from here and our language isn't understood. And now she's saying Latin will be spoken from the Euphrates to the Pillars of Hercules.

FIRST CITIZEN: Madness!

THIRD CITIZEN: Why should we care? Why should we be interested how people are going to speak hundreds of years from now?

SACRIFICULUS: She has prophesied that a new religion will come from the East, where a holy man will smash the idols of the gods and then, what she and Antistius call 'the Divinity', will be worshipped through good thoughts and deeds.

FIRST CITIZEN: The poor girl's head has been turned.

SECOND CITIZEN: You know who by!

FIRST CITIZEN: Her mind is full of confusion.

THIRD CITIZEN: You know who made her so!

SECOND CITIZEN: The world's going crazy.

FIRST CITIZEN: Carmenta tries to reconcile contradictions, to build up impossibilities, now she doesn't know where to stop. She might as well prophesy that white is black, that beauty is hideous.

SECOND CITIZEN: That's the truth! Everything's falling apart!

NARRATOR: *Now the Demagogue* CETHEGUS *enters with his* FOLLOWERS *crowding round him.*

CETHEGUS: Yes, indeed, my friends. Everything. And yet... we the common people might just be the ones to put it all back together again. The aristocracy are self-serving, puffed up with pride, leeches sucking the blood of the populace. What does it matter to them if the masses starve as long as their own granaries are full? What they call their 'values' are really class secrets passed down from blue-blooded father to privileged son to oppress true citizens. They drag us off to fight their wars which make their reputations. They boss us about and maintain that the burdens they inflict upon us are for our own good. This evil will only come to an end on the day when each and every soldier ordered to march on the foe will, in the name of true equality, turn his weapon against his real enemy: his commanding officer. Then and only then will we share this land equally between ourselves. Only when the difference between the great and the small is abolished for good and all will we ordinary folk find true happiness.

FIRST FOLLOWER: Listen to Cethegus! Hear the truth he speaks! The posh folk are leading us into war. The origin of the all the people's woes comes from the aristos. You know why they want war? Because they make a profit out of our suffering. Military prowess is just another vanity of the patriarchs, another myth of their superiority.

SECOND FOLLOWER: So true! Courage? That's another indulgence. It should be taxed like any other luxury good.

FIRST FOLLOWER: You know, I've often thought there should also be a tax on virtue. And those who have to pay most should be the do-gooders. When it comes down to it, they're the ones who enjoy being virtuous.

SECOND FOLLOWER: Here's somebody talking sense. If every one of us owned our own plot of land we'd soon be prepared to fight.

FIRST FOLLOWER: And what about charity? Those who enjoy helping others ought to have to pay for their pleasure.

SECOND FOLLOWER: Virtue. Courage. Charity. All meaningless concepts the aristocrats have made their own.

NARRATOR: TITIUS *has heard all this.*

TITIUS: This strikes me with terror. Society is founded upon truths too subtle for these plebs to appreciate. The labourer thinks he's talking sense when he says: 'I've ploughed and sown this field, so the corn that grows here should all belong to me.' And yet, nothing could be further from the truth. The peasants can't defend the land. Ultimately, the land belongs to the man who is prepared to take up arms to defend it. It's the military commanders who should be the true owners. Without them, our enemies might just as well stroll in and take our land away from us. This is what these common folk never seem to understand: they would be completely exposed without the protection of organised military force.

CETHEGUS: So the general is to be our master? Then our master is our enemy. When it comes to battle our share is suffering and death while he gets all the glory. We're not that stupid! Patronage is just another word for slavery. Why should slaves have to defend a system which grants them no rights? The patriarchs speak of avenging the defeat of Alba Longa ten years ago. What I say is it was never the likes of me who was beaten. Those walls we see every day rising up there on the horizon in Rome which cause our aristocrats such grief, what do they matter to us? The enemy of our enemy is our friend. Sure enough, it'll be hard to put up with the pride of the conqueror. But the disdain of a stranger will be easier to accept than the contempt of our own leaders.

LIBERALIS: Cethegus, don't you see that your values run the risk of destroying all patriotic sentiments in the hearts of the people? Yours is still an Alban heart. Have some humility! Join those of us who serve the cause of liberty and progress. Are you not moved by the fine example of Antistius?

CETHEGUS: Not in the least, Liberalis. As far as I'm concerned Antistius is no better than any other of the idle rich. How does he spend his time? Thinking great thoughts which he puts into the mouth of Carmenta. Do they give the people any inspiration? You heard her latest claptrap: 'The language of Latium will spread to the ends of the earth.' Another doctrine which will surely result in the deaths of thousands! What good will it do us to have our language spoken all over the globe if our bones are rotting under the ground? 'We will civilise the world!' Oh, really? 'We will establish justice!' Who for? Will this new justice bring any benefit to the likes of us? We'll end up starving once again, with the patrician foot on our neck.

LIBERALIS: Can't you see that Antistius is developing a religion which is so much purer than any philosophy humanity has ever known?

CETHEGUS: And what has that to do with us? Like every other priest he's only in it for what he can get out of it. Caterpillar or butterfly, it's still the same insect.

LIBERALIS: You say you work for the good of the people, Cethegus. Your people are all true believers. Yet you reject a progressive priest who wants to purify religion.

CETHEGUS: Shame on you! The people only cling to superstition because the nobility have brainwashed them.

When these 'sacred rites' are no longer shoved down their throats they'll soon see the error of their ways and spit on the altars.

LIBERALIS: But what about morality, goodness, virtue…?

CETHEGUS: More meaningless words! More superstitious nonsense. When we're the bosses things are going to be very different. The gods and their priests… maybe they'll be the last of the tyrants we'll have to get rid of… but get rid of them we will. Antistius is soft in the head. Out of touch with reality. Behind the times and ahead of the times at the same time. Not a very safe position to be in!

FIRST CITIZEN: Poor Antistius!

SECOND CITIZEN: He's finished. Both the aristocrats and the populace are against him.

VOLTINIUS: Carmenta is his greatest problem. Her ridiculous oracular insanities will end up ruining everything. Political dreams are the most fatal dreams of all. Those who fantasise about some transcendent future are the country's own worst enemy.

NARRATOR: TERTIUS *addresses the* BOURGEOISIE *of Alba.*

TERTIUS: Hold to the land, citizens. That's the way to ensure power will never fail. The principal skill of the statesman resides in his intellect, knowing the art of what is and what is not possible – that's what separates him from the herd. As far as I'm concerned, there's nothing more dangerous than imagination. I keep constant guard against the deceptions of those dreamers who claim to be enlightened. I rely upon objective facts, matters which are as clear as day. For instance, the prophecy of this crazed Carmenta that there will come a day when all the world will be speaking Latin and that a religion of so-called righteousness will come from the East... These latest oracles of hers are reason enough to reject everything else she's ever come out with. Let me tell you this, alone among all the other statesmen, I was never taken in. I've always showed good sense. I never allowed myself to be duped by any fantasy.

FIRST BOURGEOIS: Well said, Tertius. This man's got his head screwed on. He has the soul of sense inside the hide of a buffalo.

SECOND BOURGEOIS: And he's a true patriot to boot. He won't be fooled by these tales of the destiny of Rome. He's all for Alba. He only wants what's honourable for us from Alba Longa.

THIRD BOURGEOIS: Hear, hear! As far as I'm concerned, the worst crime of Antistius and Carmenta is that that they're always taking the side of Rome. No-one should be allowed make the enemy's case for them.

LIBERALIS: Should we not, at least, make our own case? Who's to say that the spirit of Latium does not reside in Carmenta? The voice of the Sybil is the voice of this land. I for one cannot hear her words without trembling. Her oracle that: 'The language of Latium will one day be the language of the whole world'. Well... who knows? The scope of possibility is far more vast than our narrow minds can comprehend.

FIRST BOURGEOIS: Come off it. There are hundreds of tongues in this world. Why would other tribes give up their own languages and start speaking ours?

SECOND BOURGEOIS: And she says it will be Rome of all places which is going to make this happen.

FIRST BOURGEOIS: For shame. The Sibyl is a traitress!

NARRATOR: *When the* PEOPLE *of all parties leave* VOLTINIUS *and* TITIUS *are left alone.*

VOLTINIUS: I'm telling you, Titius: a nation is lost when it concerns itself with anything other than patriotism. Social questions, religious questions... all this analysis, all this self-scrutiny draws so much blood from the vital force of our fatherland.

TITIUS: We could die by living too much, just as we could by living too little.

VOLTINIUS: I believe Alba will die by asking too many questions.

TITIUS: That's a disease which is very slow to kill.

SCENE TWO.

NARRATOR: *The Temple of Nemi is built on a rock over-hanging the lake surrounded by the deep, sacred wood. The Oracle comes out of a cleft in the rock.* GANEO *and* SACRIFICULUS, *Servers at the Temple, are seated outside.*

SACRIFICULUS: Have you ever noticed, Ganeo, how the tastes of the gods seem to vary according to the whims of their priests? You must have noticed how our mighty goddess seems strangely indulgent towards her priest Antistius? In the old days at this sanctuary the more dreadful and bloody the rites performed by the priests the more devout and pious those priests were considered. Now, our stern Diana has become so feminine that she wants her temple to be more like a women's sewing circle. I have to go along with it. But it strikes me that the number of sacrifices hasn't half gone down.

GANEO: I know what you mean. The gods lose their divine power as soon as their believers stop fearing them. We should never mess with their powers. Diana is not a goddess to be worshipped with games and laughter. She's not Venus. Wasn't it always drummed into us servers at the temple that sacrificial offerings are the very basis of our faith, and that the day we stop offering sacrifices everything will go to ruin?

NARRATOR: ANTISTIUS *comes from inside the Temple.*

ANTISTIUS: Wash away, wash away from the temple the last hideous trace of blood! Should any uncorrupted flesh remain, give it to feed the poor. I beg you to purge yourselves of the abominable belief that the Divinity takes pleasure in the slaughter of the shambles.

NARRATOR: POOR PEOPLE *approach and* SACRIFICULUS *and* GANEO *try to drive them away.*

SACRIFICULUS: Get out of here!

ANTISTIUS: Don't send them away! Come near, come near, my children! What was offered to the gods is now all yours. True sacrifice is when we give away what belongs to ourselves to the poor and needy.

GANEO: What do you reckon to all this, Sacrificulus? Have you ever heard the like?

SACRIFICULUS: My faith, no! It seems that now we have to welcome with open arms all the riff-raff we used to drive away.

GANEO: Everything changes! A new congregation for new gods!

NARRATOR: ANTISTIUS *stops before the peristylum of the Temple.*

ANTISTIUS: No more gods. Only the Divinity – a Divinity which takes no pleasure from crime and injustice. Human folly should never be allowed to prevail against divine truth. You have worshipped passionate, greedy, selfish, immoral gods – such gods do not exist. Any gods which could be appeased and won over by gifts, rather than by goodness and virtue, should be brought down, even if they were to exist. The best way to pay homage to this dark, cruel Diana is to deny her very existence. But you chaste, solemn shade of our forest, you do exist and I love you. I refuse to believe that a wicked, bloody spirit dwells on the shores of this lake and within these lovely woods, which are as old as the world, dying each year only to be born again all by themselves. What moves me within this sacred grove is not fear, but love. I can find no place for fear anywhere in nature. Our forefathers were awed by nature because they were ignorant. Bountiful nature will smile upon us, as long as we, guided by wisdom, learn how to control and make use of her manifold gifts.

These gods are an affront to the Godhead. Thou Supreme Being who giveth life to all and who holdeth all within thee, I bow before thee. The dark waters of the lake of Nemi praise thee. What art thou? Thou art the first cause of reason and love in this world. Whenever men would seek to glorify thy holy name through acts of hatred and death, they blaspheme against thee. Thou art the genesis of all living things and in thee all living things are bound as one together. Whenever I preach love and brotherhood I know I am thy true priest!

Far from being an apostate from the age-old vocation of the

priests of Latium, I am certain it is I who am truly faithful and who will ensure the continuation of this temple. You ancient priests, I honour and respect you. You did what you had to in your age of iron. Even though what you taught was in error, I cannot believe you were ever deliberately deceitful. But I would be truly dishonest were I to proclaim teachings I now know to be harmful and wrong. In your day you were the zealous guardians of goodness and truth. That which you once were, I now must be. The sacred tradition of the past fights against those who would gainsay this today. Let the secret voice of this prophetic soil continue to speak to me as once it spoke to my predecessors!

These gods are an affront to the Godhead. And the Godhead, in his turn, will be an affront to the Divinity. The gods are wilful, selfish, small-minded. And the one God who will come after them will doubtless often be wilful, selfish and small-minded. Men are sacrificed to gods we have created out of our ignorance and lack of understanding. Men will continue to be sacrificed to the one God we will create out of our reason. Actions the common folk now ascribe to the gods, will one day be attributed by so-called enlightened theologians to the one God. No! No! The Godhead does not respond to appeals from the will of man any more than the old false gods have ever done.

Prayer is futile. Oh blind humanity, you envisage the Divinity as a judge you can influence and win over by your demands. You imagine Eternal Reason can be swayed by your entreaties. But even if there were a God who could hear these supplications, his first duty would be to chastise you for making them. For the first duty of a judge is to throw out of court any supplicant who attempts to affect his judgment through bribes and solicitations. Hold your tongue, vile beggar! Respect the eternal order of the universe and conduct your life in obedience to its laws. Turn your eyes towards the heavens! Look ever upward!

There will always be those who come to worship at the sacred shrine of Nemi. This holy ground is stained with blood, but the day will come when only tears will mingle with the solemn waters of this lake. Tears are the eternal sacrifice, the holy libation, the stream of the soul. Oh infinite joy! How sweet it is to weep!

NARRATOR: *Noises are heard approaching.* GANEO *ushers in the* HERNICIAN DELEGATION *with their* PRISONERS, *arms bound and ready for sacrifice.*

GANEO: Your Holiness, the Hernicians have sent a delegation duty bound to offer a solemn sacrifice to the goddess.

LEADER OF THE DELEGATION: Dread priest of the goddess, following the great scourges which have ravaged our land, we consulted the oracle our forefathers have always obeyed and it has ordered us to sacrifice five men to the mighty goddess here at her terrible lake. We therefore bring you these youths. Here they are: handsome, good and strong; young men, to be sure, as we are required to bestow as a worthy offering to the gods. Slay them yourself or else give the order for their bodies to be tossed into the abyss of doom.

ANTISTIUS: Cursed be that oracle which has inspired you to offer such votives! How can you believe there could be any deity so perverse as to take delight in the blood of poor murdered creatures?

LEADER OF THE DELEGATION: What are you saying? Our forefathers have always observed the words of the soothsayers. The oracle and our adherence to the temple of Nemi constitute the bond of the Hernicians with the league of Latium. Would you rather we sided with the Volscians?

> These men are content to die. Do as your office demands!

ANTISTIUS: Never! Poor victims, given as a deadly offering by blameworthy bigotry, you must live! I free you from your bonds. From now on venerate the only true faith: that of justice and reason.

FIRST PRISONER: What can this mean? As far as we're concerned we're already dead.

SECOND PRISONER: We thought the goddess had need of our blood.

THIRD PRISONER: What strange words are these?

FOURTH PRISONER: What is this justice, this reason?

FIFTH PRISONER: What new sort of priest is this?

GANEO: Evidently nobody told you that for some time now the rites at this temple have been messed about with. But don't worry; Sacrificulus and me still keep up the good old customs.

NARRATOR: SACRIFICULUS *and* GANEO *open a door leading out onto a precipice above the lake. Corpses hang from the rock, blood stains are all around and a pile of bones lie on the ground. Aided by the members of the delegation they throw the five prisoners into the abyss, then shut the door.*

SACRIFICULUS: Well, there's five new recruits to Antistius's squadron of justice and reason.

GANEO: Not that they seemed especially grateful to him. What's he think he's playing at?

LEADER OF THE DELEGATION: He's a fool. It's not the happiest task in the world to have to deliver up victims for sacrifice. They don't thank you for it. But it has to be done. The way we've been treated at this temple doesn't exactly make us want to come back in a hurry. Perhaps in future we might be better off with the Volscians. They have mysteries every bit as terrible as once were here. A stern, traditional folk, they are.

NARRATOR: *The Delegation leaves.* GANEO *brings in* MATERNA.

GANEO: Priest, here's a poor woman who wants to speak to you on behalf of her sick son.

MATERNA: Holy Father, I'll do anything I have to, I'll pay you everything you ask, if my boy, my sole support, my only hope, may be saved.

ANTISTIUS: Keep your offerings. Or share them with those who are even worse off than yourself. How dare you believe that the Divinity would over-turn the order of nature for the sake of such lowly votives you could bestow?

MATERNA: What! You will do nothing to save my son? You evil man! My boy will die and it will be all your fault. What use is the greatest temple in the world if a priest such as you presides here?

NARRATOR: *She leaves and* VIRGINIA *and* VIRGINIUS *enter tentatively.*

VIRGINIA: Holy Father, we were tending our flocks…

VIRGINIUS: Side by side on the slopes of Mount Lucretilus…

VIRGINIA: When we fell madly in love…

VIRGINIUS: Together we both learnt of love for the very first time…

VIRGINIA: Sharing a desire which yet remains pure…

VIRGINIUS: We have heard about the goddess of this temple…

VIRGINIA: This steadfast virgin who loves the virginal…

VIRGINIUS: So we're bringing these two doves as our votive offering for sacrifice…

VIRGINIA: To beseech you, dear priest, to grant a favourable augury for our union.

ANTISTIUS: My children, my children, this temple was built for such as you. Enter the sanctum sanctorum. But, please, open your cage and let these birds fly free. Offer the goddess the only gift which will please her: a pure heart.

> Oh sacred enchantment of nature, love which absorbs us all, yours is the perfect voice, the proof that can never deceive. Yes, there is an unknown god in whom we must believe. Shame on those who would make light of such a mystery! Shame on those who would look down upon the lowliest of persons attempting to fulfil the supreme act of the human spirit. Oh Venus, mother of the race of Aeneas, exquisite heavenly delight of gods and mortals, brood on these two swan's eggs, these two youngsters who have saved their first kiss for each other; allow them to form a link in that great chain of the Latin race which will one day encircle the whole world.

Love one another, my children. Stay faithful unto death.

VIRGINIA: Good priest! You will surely be our minister for ever.

VIRGINIUS: If all priests were like you they would be the father confessors of all humanity.

NARRATOR: *The young lovers go into the temple as a deputation of the* AEQUICOLAE *arrives.*

LEADER OF THE DEPUTATION: Dread priest, for so long we of the tribe of Aequicola have been parted from the league of Latium. We are deeply divided and no longer know where to turn. We have consulted our oracle which has told us to come and seek you out; such is the great reputation of the wisdom of the priests of this temple. We Aequicolae must have a new constitution and be allied once more. We are prepared to supply any number of victims necessary to secure the aid of the goddess. Priest, perform your rites. Let this honoured temple form the bond which will again attach us to the ancient confederation.

ANTISTIUS: You think mass slaughter will confer wisdom upon a nation unable to find peace within itself? Rather than consulting this oracle you should have taken heed of the spirit of your forefathers. Practice justice. Respect the rights of man. Let virtue and reason rule as the supreme divinity.

LEADER OF THE DEPUTATION: Allow me to point out, Priest of Nemi, that we don't need a representative of the gods to come out with platitudes. If this were simply a question of reason our own common sense could fathom out what to do. We have no shortage of wise men. But ultimate authority resides with the gods and they demand that traditional sacrifices should be made to them. Perform your sacred rites. Do you want the sacrificial victims to be animal? Or human? The more you ask of us, the more we will thank you, for the tougher your demands the more certain they will produce the desired effect. Come on! This is the first time we've seen a priest dithering at the prospect of a sacrifice.

ANTISTIUS: You wish for the establishment of the rule of justice, yet you wish to inaugurate it with a crime. As the first clause of your constitution you would inscribe a lie. Go somewhere else! This is no place for falsehood.

LEADER OF THE DEPUTATION: We can't understand your language. Could it be that this once flourishing sanctuary exists no longer? This shrine should be the foundation of the power of Latium. The league will be overthrown. Rome will be the new heart of the world. We will be ruled from the Capitol.

NARRATOR: *They go. The Priest is left alone.*

ANTISTIUS: This is what happens when I attempt to serve justice and reason. Even those I try to help turn their backs. Even those unfortunate souls I have done my best to deliver from the bonds of death scorn me. Has it really been worth all this trouble, devoting myself to the salvation of a contemptible mob fatally addicted to lies?

I'm tearing myself apart! If only my work might do some good to someone, to something! But before me all I see is a thankless land and a cheerless sky. Oh faith, oh hope, why have you forsaken me?

For myself, I bade farewell to the folly and delusion of past times with no regret. What liberation, what deliverance! No sense of emptiness. Only life. And yet… must I conclude that mankind needs simple certainty, a god who exists to do our bidding? Mankind needs to define the infinite. He needs to say 'Oh, my God!'; he needs a universe created in his own image where he can converse with the Absolute as if the pair of them were on equal footing, as if this god were his own best friend. He would commune with the Ideal as if it were no different from himself. He wants to ask favours, give thanks and fool himself that the Supreme Being takes a blind bit of notice.

If only one day our imagination might create a different kind of god! If myths told in temples might be transformed into tales of a human life, of someone who goes through this world doing good. Minds would be turned by such a new god! Humanity demands from its gods that they should be both finite and infinite, real and ideal at the same time. They purport to love the Ideal – but only if can be personified, only if God can be, at the same time, Man. What they want is a Superman… that would satisfy them! The never-ending swell of the oceans is as of nothing when compared to the waves of illusion human beings will have to swim through before they arrive at something which bears any resemblance to reason.

How fortunate is he who dwelleth in the eye of the storm, succoured by a raven who bringeth quotidian repast. Man's stupidity makes moral isolation the lot of those who outstrip their fellows by head and heart. Would it not be better for me to let them fulfil their fate, to abandon them to the wrongful errors they cling to so fondly? No! There is reason. Reason still exists within the heart of man. Whoever loves reason must also love mankind, because reason can only exist in the mind of man. So I must create my own tiny divine world, garbing myself in the robes of the infinite. Just as simple people say: 'Oh, my God', I must be able to swear: 'Oh, my

Infinite'. Perhaps it is those two innocents, Virginia and Virginius, who best understand that we can come close to God only through love. Oh universal reason! I know in my heart that in seeking whatsoever is good, whatsoever is true, I struggle for thee!

I'm all alone. Even poor Carmenta doesn't understand.

NARRATOR: *A sound is heard, announcing the approach of the Sybil.* CARMENTA *enters clad in a black dress. She has long black hair, tied up with red ribbons.*

CARMENTA: Here I am, your poor daughter, dragging her deceiving frame through the cloisters of this cursed temple. Only twenty-two years old, yet veiled and shrouded in the black robes of an old woman. But look into these tender little eyes, like drowning stars lost in their deep orbits. Is my fate always to be tied to vows I never wished to take? You who are the wisest of the wise, you who deliver your followers from burdens inflicted upon them by the past, will you not spare a moment of pity for me? Will you not declare the Sibyl to be a woman like any other? Free me to be a woman and a mother. Allow me to deck my breast with flowers, to plait my heavy locks. You know very well that you yourself could pronounce those oracles you make me say. You could be the voice of all those truths which will save the people.

ANTISTIUS: Dearest daughter, each one of us is chained to our duty. We must not say: 'My lot is hard, my share is heavy.' To work for humanity demands submission and surrender. In battle a soldier cannot say to his comrade: 'My post is too perilous – you take it.' We live and die where fate has placed us.

CARMENTA: So we two must be the exception to your law of

love. You will free every captive except ourselves.

ANTISTIUS: None of us can be released from our duty. No revolution can liberate us from the obligations of the universal purpose. The only vows that can be broken are the ones that mean nothing. Promises made to country, to honour, to duty, can never be rendered null and void. By virtue of your illustrious birth you were dedicated to one of the offices which define us as Latins: you are the Sibyl; you are bound to serve. This is where you belong. Even if the gods to whom you made your vows do not exist, a Divinity does exist. What would happen if there ever came a day when the sacred maid of Latium became a woman like any other and lost her holy halo of virginity? I am a priest and will remain a priest for as long as I live. I have the right – no, it is my duty – to ensure that religion evolves and progresses in every way possible. But I have no right to destroy religion entirely. I must never cease to be a priest. No-one will ever see Antistius in any other role than that of the master of the sacred rites. And no-one should ever see you profane the calling of Sibyl. The demands of our country have decreed you must be a crazed outsider. There's no cure for a being such as you who has been consecrated to the gods. In another life your beauty might have aroused so much love. Too bad! You must taste death without having aroused any feeling other than terror.

CARMENTA: Why must I wear this unbearable mask! Forgive me if I desire to taste real life. I would gladly die for the truth you preach, so how can you, in all conscience, force me to lie?

ANTISTIUS: No, no! I have never told you to speak anything but the truth. The world is led by prophets, by those who know how to see the effect in the cause. The Sibyl can never be a liar, can never be mistaken. The Sibyl is the voice of

Latium, the guide of our race, revelatrix of our destinies. Each race creates its own destiny. The Sibyl sees and makes her pronouncements. As the strong do not deceive when they assert their strength so the mystic does not lie when she reveals her clairvoyance.

Look down there, past the shores of the lake, down to the port of Antium washed by the sea. Ships of the Phoenicians bring us trinkets; triremes of the Greeks bring us luxuries. But moral strength... where will that come from? What will bring goodness into this disordered world: the axe or the sword? Yes, I believe in our own people. One day the whole of Italy will be Latin and the whole world will bow down to us.

CARMENTA: When that day dawns I will have been long forgotten. No-one will remember poor Carmenta.

ANTISTIUS: Surely that is so. Would you want the prophet to be as immortal as her oracle? You won't be treated any worse than the millions of other creatures sacrificed by Nature to her own great purpose.

CARMENTA: But you have often said that Alba is finished, that these old heaps of lava which form our mountains will see its splendour transplanted elsewhere.

ANTISTIUS: Yes, this change will surely come. Others will have that privilege. Alba will die; but Rome will live and will accomplish what Alba should have done.

CARMENTA: When I pronounce such thoughts from the mouth of the oracle I see the eyes of those who hear flash with fury.

ANTISTIUS: Men become passionate for their own little cause

because they do not see the whole of the picture.

CARMENTA: Father, when I am with you and I hear your words, even though I don't always understand them, I sense I must be ready to make any sacrifice. I accept my destiny, hard as it may be. But whenever I am not upheld by your regard, I weaken. To be selected for a holy vocation might be good for a man, but for a woman it's so cruel. What consolation can she take when the common pleasures of life are denied her?

ANTISTIUS: And yet it is woman who must set the example of faith and duty to the world. Carmenta, your chaste black robes will become the symbol of a noble female company who will find in religion a means of fulfilling their duty in chastity and the dignity of life.

Woman will understand far better than man that life is meaningless without obligation and the spiritual fruits that follow in its wake.

CARMENTA: Then we will do what you wish. But you must support us; you must love us and let us know we are loved by you. Woman will never do good without the love of man. Would you condemn us for that?

ANTISTIUS: Dearest daughters of the sex I love, how could I blame you for the very quality which gives you your power? Woman must love man, and man must love God. Everything great in the service of the Ideal must be accomplished through men and women working together. The sacred work to which I am devoted is the expulsion of false gods. This can only lead to my death. But it will finally be accomplished when women at last rebel against these evil and impure practices undeserving of the name of religion. Nothing will be achieved in this world until men and women work together, before the marriage of reason and constant faith.

CARMENTA: And so you love me and allow me to love you?

ANTISTIUS: My dear daughter, love is a goddess worshipped under many names. Virginius and Virginia, the young lovers who came here, they love in a way sanctified and blessed by Nature. On every rung of the endless ladder love transforms the world and oils the wheels of the universe. Everything that is good and beautiful is formed from the same principle as the attraction of one for another. Orpheus would still have been the most perfect lover, even if he had never known Eurydice. If you want my opinion, Eurydice limited him, it's a pity she ever crossed his path. What role can a woman play in the life of someone whose mission is to save and to civilise his fellows? A messenger of the divine, like Orpheus, should be loved without having to love. A woman should merely be permitted to wash his feet and kiss the hem of his garment.

CARMENTA: That will have to suffice. Only let us know that you look upon us with favour. What more can we ask? Take me; direct me; rebuke me, so that I feel you are my master. Each word that comes from your lips, I will repeat. You will be my conscience, my soul; I will kneel at your feet. But I live in a frozen world under a sorrowful sky. No-one casts a loving eye upon me; I have no spouse, no-one to look up to… Forgive me. I must be resigned. Tell me, father, do you ever spare a thought for Carmenta? Do I mean anything to you?

ANTISTIUS: Your heart is true, even when your judgment is flawed. At the core and depth of every woman is a sweet fondness which must be assuaged by tender words and caresses.

CARMENTA: Restore me; correct me. A man like you could never be possessed completely. It will have to suffice to obey you. Only, what I have of you, I want to have all to myself, to myself alone, do you see? I'm jealous, understand?

ANTISTIUS: Every man wants to carve out a place in the universe which is his alone. Every woman wants to have a part of a man which is hers alone. The Infinite hovers over us and looks down with indulgence. This work is so demanding! How can I try to extract an iota of devotion from a solid mass of selfishness? How can I tell the world that this is what it needs?

CARMENTA: Don't you ever sometimes have doubts? At night when you close your eyes on the sight of this lake and these woods, don't you ever regret your life of dedication? Don't you ever wish for the human life you turned your back on? What reward do you find in renunciation?

ANTISTIUS: I don't know... and I don't want to know. I serve goodness, that's all I'm sure of. That one idea makes a man divine. It inspires me. It fills me with the infinite.

CARMENTA: Then that must be your reward. But isn't it only fair that I should have one too? You have the certainty of doing good. All I have for my reward is your smile. Is that enough? I will suffer anything you ask of me. But you could thank me for it, couldn't you?

ANTISTIUS: *(planting a kiss on her forehead)* Sister, I love you... in duty and in martyrdom.

CARMENTA: Now use me as you see fit, even unto death. Tell me what to do. Your Sibyl will never cast off her robes of black. I will say whatever words inspire you for the love of truth and in the best interests of the people of Latium.

My black-clad sisters, I see you in the future! If ever there should come those who would force you to lift your veil, even in the name of reason, you must refuse to be free; you must keep faith with your funereal vows. Shame on her who would convert to common sense after tasting holy folly! The only vow forever binding is Divine madness!

SCENE THREE.

NARRATOR: METIUS *and* VOLTINIUS *meet in the atrium of the House of Metius in Alba.*

METIUS: Believe me, Voltinius, there's no more time to be lost. Each day another stone falls from the ancient edifice of Alba. We're being torn apart by religious divisions, social crises; patriotism itself is in doubt; more and more of the people are coming to believe that there can be no worse fate than dying for their country. Antistius's reformations, his futile attempts to establish a rational religion, are destabilising the republic. Disorder is everywhere and, in the last analysis, it's all our fault.

Woe unto an aristocracy which conceives that our ancient titles give us a right to be idle! We aristocrats are not here to rest on our laurels, but to dare. We must save Alba, and to save our state we must plunge the people into cold water and force upon them something they don't want to do: to take a strong stand. War! That's the only way to stifle these social uncertainties. War confers rank upon the brave; war affirms the status of those who have the right to be leaders of society. War rewards the courage of the few over the many. War demonstrates the necessity for virtue. Might is the true measure of what is right.

VOLTINIUS: You're saying we should declare war? Against whom?

METIUS: Against Rome, of course. Does Alba have any other enemies?

VOLTINIUS: Why should we go to war now?

METIUS: Because we are already on the back foot. A nation is formed from pride, self-assertion… arrogance if you will. A humble nation is already defeated.

VOLTINIUS: Then a nation has to behave like a bully boy?

METIUS: Naturally. The very qualities which would be vile in an individual make a nation great. A nation is a creature of glory; it gorges on glory; glory succours it. A defeated nation has no life. Revenge is the enduring drive of a nation. If Alba waits any longer she will be finished. Better to die young of a mortal wound than to fade away like a tired old man.

VOLTINIUS: You're forgetting two things: first, the democratic faction holds the whip hand in our country and you know what they think of the military…

METIUS: That's of scant consequence. A democracy's main problem is that its leadership can never do what it really wants. In a democracy the leaders have to respond to public opinion, they're unable to resist the passions of the moment. This democratic faction is essentially pacifist. But who knows? It could well become the party which might most easily embark upon war. Take Liberalis for instance, he's in power and he's the greatest of pacifists. Oh, he's such a great peace-monger! But maybe things might turn out so that Liberalis will end up as the leader in a war he himself opposes. Rather than ceding power to his opposition, he'd end up doing the very last thing he wants.

VOLTINIUS: But secondly, Rome seems to be showing an unprecedented degree of moderation towards us right now… though I'll make no predictions about the future.

METIUS: True enough, maybe Rome is not preparing to attack us at this moment. Rome is a young tiger whose teeth are still growing. Its walls are scarcely built; the right elements are not yet all in place. But as a rule, war arises not from volition, but from unforeseeable circumstances. Believe me, before too many days have passed we will have war.

VOLTINIUS: You want war and you'll do whatever it takes to make sure we get it. But you contradict yourself. Explain this to me: You condemn the people for their lack of militaristic zeal, yet at the same time you seem to be saying that they could become so besotted with war that they would drive their leader to battle even though that's the last thing he wants?

METIUS: Both those propositions are true at the same time. The masses are incapable of understanding the advantages of military rule and they're always suspicious of any general who comes to power through victorious exploits on the battlefield. Nevertheless, they'll always support a war if they think they can get something out of it. War puts an end to the daily grind; it makes life more interesting. Some men even enjoy military service, provided they're not on the front line; joining up gives them the satisfaction of claiming they're playing their part in safeguarding the fatherland. How wonderful to be a hero if you manage to survive… and at so much a day all found! War is a time of contentment for those who have nothing to lose… and who might even come out better off by pillaging the enemy's possessions.

And, even if they're on the losing side, these ill-fated heroes can always raise their voices against their leaders and blame them for their betrayal.

NARRATOR: *A* SERVANT *enters.*

SERVANT: I bring news, your lordships. This morning at Bovilles, some young men from Alba were out celebrating a family feast, their heads covered with caps of flowers, when they picked a fight with a bunch of Romans who happened to be passing. Five or six of our boys were killed.

METIUS: What did I tell you, Voltinius?

VOLTINIUS: We have to find out who started it. A thorough enquiry will determine which side is in the wrong and whether our lads acted honourably.

SERVANT: Naturally, both sides are claiming it was the other who started it. The citizens are all wound up and flocking to the forum.

METIUS: We better see what's going on.

SCENE FOUR.

NARRATOR: CITIZENS *are gathering at the Forum of Alba when* VOLTINIUS *and* METIUS *arrive.*

FIRST CITIZEN: The question is: What's best? To lay down our lives or suffer outrages worse than death?

SECOND CITIZEN: That's right! Death or infamy?

CITIZENS: War! To Rome!

VOLTINIUS: Wait… please! Take care. You're not ready. For the last ten years Rome has been dedicated to the sole aim of perfecting its military prowess… while you have let yours fall into decline. Don't rush into this!

THIRD CITIZEN: Who is this treacherous citizen? Kill him! Burn his house down!

FIRST CITIZEN: Discouraging patriotism is the worst act of a traitor.

NARRATOR: LIBERALIS *arrives with his followers.*

LIBERALIS: Citizens! The mark of a free people is being able to weigh up our actions with all due care and consideration for the consequences. Now, I have no desire to anticipate the investigation into this morning's regrettable incident…

FIRST CITIZEN: No need for an investigation.

SECOND CITIZEN: We all know what happened.

LIBERALIS: Even supposing the evidence is clear, should we involve the Republic of Alba in a conflict which can only result in the destruction of a constitution you all wished for? This war will be our ruin. Alba has been beaten twice in the past ten years. If we lose again our city will be wiped off the face of history. And if we win… your new ruler will be a victorious general, an imperator.

THIRD CITIZEN: Why not? We can't be any worse off than we already are!

LIBERALIS: Is that what you want: a military dictatorship?

That would mean the death of the republic.

NARRATOR: *A loud noise is heard as a procession sweeps into the Forum carrying five blood-stained corpses. Extraordinary emotion from the crowd as* LIBERALIS *tries to speak.*

FIRST CITIZEN: Enough of your talk! To arms!

CITIZENS: Vengeance! To Rome! To Rome!

NARRATOR: CETHEGUS *speaks to his followers in a low voice.*

CETHEGUS: Leave them be. However this turns out it will be the ruin of the Liberals.

NARRATOR: *Now* METIUS *comes forward and stills the Crowd.*

METIUS: Citizens! All our past differences should now be over. This is a question of the honour of the fatherland.

FIRST CITIZEN: At last somebody's talking sense.

SECOND CITIZEN: Something to be said for these old aristocrats… Sometimes.

METIUS: Is it we who are declaring war? No, it's already been declared by an act of provocation. And I for one am ready to give up everything I have for the sake of the fatherland.

CITIZENS: Bravo, bravo, Metius!

LIBERALIS: Allow me one word…

CETHEGUS: We already know what you're going to say, Liberalis, you spineless leader of a faction that's brought us nothing but disgrace. *(to the Crowd)* The only counsel this shifty, lying politician has ever offered is cowardice. That's what's led us to our present miserable state. Very well, if Liberalis and his pards are so keen to forsake the honour of Alba, then it's up to us to defend it. These bastards have ground the fatherland into the mud. It's up to us, citizens, to drag it out of the mire.

NARRATOR: LIBERALIS *confers with his Supporters.*

LIBERALIS: You know if we give up now it'll be the triumph of insanity. Our patriotism demands we stand firm.

FOLLOWER OF LIBERALIS: Don't worry. We will. We're with you, Liberalis. *(to the Crowd)* Let him speak! Let Liberalis speak!

CITIZENS: What's the use? No! Shut up!

LIBERALIS: If those who are trying to silence me would allow me to put my point across to my people for a moment… Perhaps I could take this opportunity to explain that what seems to be dividing us is entirely based upon a misunderstanding. It's true I've always been against going to war. I'm not ashamed of that. I've done everything in my power to prevent war. But now, it would seem we no longer have any option. I promise you that from now on I will be every bit as dedicated to warfare as I once was devoted to the cause of peace.

CITIZENS: That's what we want to hear! Good for you!

TITIUS: So there we have it – this time yesterday nobody wanted war and now everyone's all for it.

METIUS: *(triumphant)* What did I tell you, Voltinius?

VOLTINIUS: *(whispering)* You scoundrel, Metius. You know better than anyone that our defeat is certain.

METIUS: Citizens, to Rome!

CITIZENS: To Rome! To Rome!

VOLTINIUS: How can you do this? Manipulating the crowd, playing on their prejudices. You ought to know that war is brutal and the victors are the greatest of the brutes. The best thing in this world is liberty. But in war liberty amounts to weakness. In war every true virtue counts for nothing. What you call warlike virtues are nothing but vices. True virtue, civilisation, everything that is good, gentle, nurturing… what has that to do with men hacking each other to death?

METIUS: You still don't understand do you, Voltinius? The role of the people is to suffer. Humans are born in chains, banging their heads against the prison walls.

CITIZENS: To Rome! To Rome!

SCENE FIVE.

NARRATOR: *At the Temple of Nemi* ANTISTIUS *stands by the lake in contemplation.*

ANTISTIUS: Impossible to escape from the triple conundrum of a moral life: God, Justice, Immortality! Virtue has no need of human justice; but virtue cannot dispense with a celestial witness to say: 'Courage, courage!' Oh Death which I see approaching, Death which I summon, Death which I embrace, I only wish you could be of some use to someone somewhere, even at the furthest limits of the infinite.

NARRATOR: LIBERALIS *enters suddenly.*

LIBERALIS: My priest, the time for action is upon us. A terrible wrong has been committed which is none of our making, but which can only be put right by us. In any hands other than yours and mine war against Rome would be the final catastrophe. Help me limit the evil. But first we must win. The oracle is in your hands. Convince the people that those heavenly voices, which have hitherto been on the side of Rome, are now no longer. These folk are going forth to be killed for the sake of their fatherland; you must give them some reason to die.

ANTISTIUS: How can you expect me to curse those who are blessed by the spirit of Latium? The duty to die is always clear: we can only stay in our proper place. I am ready to set the example.

LIBERALIS: That means nothing to me. People like you imagine you've done your bit for society when, having destroyed ordinary instincts for the right in human consciousness, you reckon you can look yourself in the eye and believe you've set nothing but a good example. Take care your faith that the gods are watching over you is not built on a lie. Your philosophy provides a justification for being killed; why can't it also give a validation for killing? A soldier's duty is made of both obligations: to kill and be killed. I scorn any philosophy which only inspires courage to face death without being ready to dish it out.

ANTISTIUS: Among those who give and receive death there are few who act out of any motive except passion – that's what puts strength into the arms of men. There must be rules to govern men when they act like wolves. You're trying to put a gloss of high morality onto actions which are the very negation of decency. That's a task for which I have little taste. Let people dispense with principles altogether; but don't give them sophistry in place of truth.

LIBERALIS: Ah, Priest of Nemi, I see your true self under the folds of your cassock. And I see what our future will be if we listen to you and your kind. The priest in linen robes and the iron-clad warrior – both stand apart from ordinary life, one in his fortress, the other in his temple. The priest, proud to represent the celestial ideal, has nothing to say to someone ready to lay down his life for an earthly city. The priest and the patriot are as opposed as two irreconcilable antitheses. Oh fatal limits of human nature! In striving for perfection must we become vile? Does your great wisdom mean you cannot give consolation to a woman, a child, a soldier? I'm almost missing Tetricus. I'm disgusted by you: a priest who has too great a horror of blood. You are no longer a man.

ANTISTIUS: Go and follow the prejudices of the class that forged you. As for me, I will follow my own fate. Never try to prevent a flower born in darkness from turning its face towards the light.

LIBERALIS: At the very least, consult your oracle, and tomorrow perform the time-honoured consecrated rites, if only out of condescension for the common people.

ANTISTIUS: *(quietly, reluctantly)* Very well... if I must.

NARRATOR: GANEO *is at the cave of the Sibyl when* PORCIA *presents herself.*

GANEO: *(aside)* When the governors go AWOL the servants must take their place. So if the Sibyl's not around, her lackey will have to speak for her. *(to Porcia)* What do you want?

PORCIA: I've come to consult the goddess to find out if the

child I bear will be a boy or girl.

GANEO: *(aside)* If I say I've no idea I'll lose my reputation. After all, if I make a guess there's a fifty-fifty chance I'll be right. And if I'm right I'll get a reward. But if I'm not then who's going to care? She won't know the outcome for a few months... Go on, let's do it! *(to Porcia)* The oracle foretells you will have a girl.

PORCIA: Oh wonderful power of the gods to reveal that which is hidden. Take this offering, minister of the gods, in thanks for the service you have rendered me.

NARRATOR: PORCIA *leaves as* LEPORINUS *enters*.

GANEO: Ah, it's you, Leporinus. You can see, my old friend, that our establishment is not exactly thriving. The way this century's turning out is beyond me. In the old days I used to understand the priests... and the sibyls. I ought to know the system round here, but these days I haven't the faintest idea what's going on. What are you up to?

LEPORINUS: The battle's about to start. I've been called up. I want to know if I'm going to be killed.

GANEO: I'll tell you. It's not hard. No need to bother the gods with that.

LEPORINUS: What!

GANEO: I'll let you in on the secret of this game. If someone asks a question like yours, the answer has to be either 'yes' or 'no'. Look at Porcia – that woman who came just now to find out if she'd have a boy or a girl – if I'd have told her the truth, which is that I don't know and I care less, she would have taken me for a fool or a knave. But if I come down one way or the other chances are evens that I won't get it wrong. If I get it right people will marvel at the spirit the Sibyl channels which can see into the future. If I get it wrong… well, it's just another entry in the catalogue of errors, which gets fuller by the day, but which nobody seems to bother too much about. In the double-entry book-keeping system of prophecy only the records accounted for on one side are cause for wonder; the others are soon forgotten. That's all there is to it. And what can be wrong with that? Everything supernatural rests on this illusion. Yes against No. Half the time you're wrong, but those times when you get it right count far more than when you place your bet on the losing side.

So you want to know whether you'll be killed in this coming war. I can say without fear of contradiction: No! Because if you are killed you won't be coming back in a hurry to tell me I was wrong. But the last thing I want is to play with the feelings of an old friend. Do you want to know something more useful?

LEPORINUS: What's that?

GANEO: What you should do so you won't be killed.

LEPORINUS: Please tell me!

GANEO: Very well. Run away!

LEPORINUS: What?

GANEO: Or make darned sure someone's killed in your place. One or the other. That's all there is to it.

LEPORINUS: That's all very well for you to say. Do you think it's that easy to slip out of the ranks with men on the right, on the left, in front and behind? How am I supposed to run away? You're squeezed together, boxed right in. The best bet is to hit out at your enemy, kill him before he can kill you. They call it military courage but mostly it's nothing but cowardice. When there's no chance of escape – to the right, to the left, to the rear – then the only thing you can do is chop your way to the front and if anybody tries to stop you, kill him, and you'll be called a hero from acting out of self-preservation. You hit the enemy not out of courage but from fear.

GANEO: You know, Leporinus, you are a very smart fellow: 'We are brave out of fear; we kill to avoid being killed.' Don't you know that's a powerful thought? And all because you're oppressed by the aristocrats who order you what to do. So in these situations maybe the best thing is to make sure it's your commander who gets beaten.

LEPORINUS: What are you talking about?

GANEO: You'll find yourself in much less danger if you make up your mind in advance to be defeated. As a general rule you're much less likely to be killed if you're on the losing side.

LEPORINUS: Eh?

GANEO: The greatest risk comes from a determination to win. You, if I'm not wrong, are not one of those fools who would be happy to be a dead hero.

LEPORINUS: My oath, no!

GANEO: I thought as much. In my book a proper champion is the one who survives. Winning is all about not getting killed. There are those who'd have us believe that a soldier who's been killed claims a share in the victory. Rubbish! Tributes piled onto the body of a dead warrior are about as much use as honouring a chopped-down tree trunk. There are those who say the Elysian Fields are set aside for fighters who died in battle. Prove it! Is the immortality of the soul reserved for soldiers alone?

LEPORINUS: Immortality reserved for the military – very droll. Mind you, at least the war dead always get great send-offs.

GANEO: Vanity of vanities.

LEPORINUS: They say the gods love the brave.

GANEO: Then bully for the gods… if they exist. I've a greater respect for my own skin than I have for the gods. Your body's going to rot in the ground whether the gods love you or not.

LEPORINUS: A dead soldier also earns the esteem of his fellow men.

GANEO: Yes, the esteem of those of your comrades in arms who were smart enough not to get killed like you. I knew two friends who lived in these parts: one was Alban the other a Volscian. When war was declared between us, five years ago, the Volscian lad came in tears to bid his friend farewell then he went and took his place in the ranks of the Volscian army… whilst our boy ran off and made himself scarce. The Volscian was killed, though his side won the battle. The Alban chap still prospers among us in perfect health. Cowardice almost always gets rewarded. As for courage, that's a virtue whose prize is death.

LEPORINUS: But don't we have to think of the nation?

GANEO: What if I were to tell you that it's in the interest of the nation to lose? Woe unto a victorious nation! The winning commander takes control and there's nobody worse, nobody more opposed to reform, than a victorious general who becomes a tyrant. But the day after defeat we're free and happy, the nation can start to progress. God preserve us from victory!

LEPORINUS: You do come out with the most contrary stuff. Fact is, I've often thought of the fate of poor little Caius, who only lived to perform heroic deeds and to brave death.

GANEO: And what happened to him?

LEPORINUS: He got himself killed on some crazy expedition against the outlaws of the Pontine Marshes.

GANEO: What an idiot! Think about it, my old pal. Leave the immortality of the soul to the soldiers and save your body. No battle can be fought without casualties. So you should make it your first aim to ensure that strategy of your general is going to fail. Generals think nothing of their poor men when they send them out on some manoeuvre where there's no chance of retreat. Then, after the common soldier gets knocked on the head and spills his guts, it's the man who gave the orders who swaggers about and gets called hero. Are you that keen, Leporinus, to make the reputation of a general at the expense of your own life?

LEPORINUS: I'm only a poor man. I can't afford grand ambitions.

GANEO: At last I'm getting through to you! Let us take pleasure in the world such as it is, my poor friend. This life is more farce than tragedy – whoever created it must have had quite a sense of humour. Having a bit of fun, that's the only theology that makes any sense in this human comedy. But if you want to enjoy yourself you have to steer clear of death. Death is a broken wheel that can't be mended. Whoever gets himself killed for one ridiculous cause or another is the greatest pillock of all. Can we help it if it's the way of the world for a man to be punished for doing good and rewarded for his evil actions?

LEPORINUS: *(thoughtful)* What if you're right, Ganeo?

GANEO: Course I'm right.

LEPORINUS: Where's Antistius?

GANEO: Down yonder, lost in thought. The poor soul's not himself today. His philosophy only works on quiet days, he has nothing to say to men who are going off to hack each other to bits. A while ago he was walking alone with his hand on his forehead, muttering: 'At time of war the immortality of the soul is a proposition of the highest necessity, for the immortality of the soul supposes the existence of the gods.' He's like a shop-keeper whose store is full of goods nobody wants. Times like these demand a level of pretence he's totally incapable of. Why did he want to become a priest? A man like him has no right to take on such an occupation if he can't fulfil the obligations. There are plenty of people around who'd like nothing more than to adopt the role of priest. I've always said we'll live to regret getting rid of Tetricus.

NARRATOR: ANTISTIUS *and* LIBERALIS *have heard all this and look at each other with fear and trembling.*

LIBERALIS: You see, Antistius? This is what goes on in the sanctuary of the goddess when her priest deserts his duties.

ANTISTIUS: Yes, truth is of use to nobody except the one who has discovered it for himself. One man's meat is another man's poison. Cursed be the divine light! Thou taughtest me how to love thee but thou hast betrayed me! I wished to perfect mankind and have only succeeded in making them worse. Joy of life, which should be the greatest principle of dignity and love, has been reduced to a sordid standard for these base wretches. They will kill me. That will be my expiation. You say men will die for chimeras. We shall see…

NARRATOR: ANTISTIUS *collapses, wiped out.* LIBERALIS *leaves.*

SCENE SIX.

NARRATOR: *At the Forum of Alba* METIUS *addresses* TITIUS.

METIUS: There comes a day, Titius, when needs must. And what we must do is put an end to all this anarchy and confusion. Our day has not yet come but the time is right to begin clearing the ground. Look, here come a bunch of blinkered democrats, my opposition. I'm their worst enemy, but watch me manipulate these layabouts so they come to believe I'm one of them.

NARRATOR: CITIZENS OF ALBA *approach* METIUS.

FIRST CITIZEN: Citizen Metius, the stand you took yesterday was much appreciated. Although you've stood apart from affairs of state for some time you voiced the true feelings of the fatherland.

METIUS: Cometh the hour cometh the man who must speak from the heart. But time is running out. We must mobilise all the vital resources of the fatherland as soon as possible. We must start with the gods. We should reverence the gods at all times, but at times of war it behoves us to be especially devout.

CITIZENS: Yes! Yes!

NARRATOR: DOLABELLA *pushes forward.*

DOLABELLA: It was the custom in times such as these to perform even more sacred rites. I have consulted the seven books of *De Jure Pontificium* and in the chapter *De religione non solum servanda sed etiam amplificanda* I read that when it comes to religion we can never do enough. To be more effective we'll need new religious practices. So I propose we send twelve young men from our best families to Etruria to learn how they worship. That should give us some new ideas.

FIRST CITIZEN: Very good! We must adopt more cults.

SECOND CITIZEN: We must increase worship for the sake of the fatherland.

METIUS: You are right, my good friends. Now let us summon the priest of our own time-honoured cult. Nothing must be neglected in propitiating the gods so they may turn their faces upon us. Above all we must be purified, we must drive from our bosom all treacherous enemies.

DOLABELLA: Propitiate the gods by sacrificing their enemies.

NARRATOR: CASCA, *a criminal, moves amongst them.*

CASCA: Let me be the one to do it!

FIRST CITIZEN: Our present priest is no true priest. He never fulfilled the essential condition of the ritual. He never killed his predecessor with his own hands. A country which forsakes religion is doomed.

SECOND CITIZEN: He's abolished the sacrifices, the very foundation of the holy terror of our cult.

THIRD CITIZEN: He ordains Carmenta to give oracles favourable to Rome.

FIRST CITIZEN: If anyone should be sacrificed to the gods it ought to be Antistius.

SECOND CITIZEN: Or Carmenta.

THIRD CITIZEN: Unhappy fate of Alba! To have such a priest at a time like this!

CASCA: I'll soon give you a new priest if you'll let me.

NARRATOR: PEASANTS *from the countryside enter the Forum, astonishing the Albans.*

FIRST PEASANT: Terrifying prodigies are all around us. The very foundations of nature and religion are shaking. I've heard about a calf born in Lanuvium yesterday without a heart – that's an obvious symbol for our Latin world where the great life-force of religion is absent. Herds in the meadows near Velletri are stubbornly refusing to eat – proof of their desire to be immolated to the glory of the gods, a privilege they've been deprived of since this impious priest has been in office. In Aricia the dogs howl woefully. And there's talk of raining stones near Proeneste.

SECOND PEASANT: Here's something I saw with my own

eyes: An ox stopped bellowing and began talking like a human being. And there were ears of corn dripping blood near Antium. Yesterday in Tusculum the sacred fowl escaped from their cages at the very moment of sacrifice and ran off into the forest – they haven't been found yet.

DOLABELLA: Surely all these marvels result from the lack of a rightful priesthood. The priest is charged to perform the sacred rites which are the foundation of the world, the basis of our stability.

FIRST COMMONER: This priest says whatever he wants. All his words, all his deeds, have the force of prayer. When he keeps telling us that it is the oracle which has decreed: 'The destiny of Latium will be realized by Rome, and through Rome Latium will conquer the world' that's hardly a good augury for us. He didn't ought to say such things... even if they turn out to be true.

DOLABELLA: Surely he is a friend of Rome. Surely he must be defrocked.

CASCA: He must be done away with.

METIUS: Let us not become divided. Antistius is still the rightful priest. We must continue to recognise him as the head of the temple which guarantees the destiny of Latium.

NARRATOR: VICTIMS, *in sacrificial garb, are ranged at the back of the Forum. As the* SERVERS *prepare to perform the sacrifice* ANTISTIUS *comes forward, supported by* LIBERALIS – *glacial silence prevails.*

ANTISTIUS: The righteous gods wish those who follow them to serve their fatherland... even when it is at fault... even when a war between the peoples of Latium is a civil war in their eyes.

A VOICE IN THE CROWD: Do you believe that our gods care anything for your sermonising? Just keep your mouth shut and carry out the rites! That's all we expect from you.

ANOTHER VOICE: Perform the ritual of blood-stained steel! Do it now!

LIBERALIS: *(whispering)* You are the priest, Antistius. You can't just stop being the priest. Do you wish to relinquish the ancient rites of Latium?

NARRATOR: *A bowl full of blood is brought. ANTISTIUS plunges the tip of a spear into it and throws it in the direction of Rome.*

VOICES: Good! At last!

A VOICE IN THE CROWD: But did you see how weakly he threw that spear towards Rome? He doesn't look like he meant it. Tetricus would've put his heart and soul into the ceremony – a proper priest was Tetricus.

DOLABELLA: In the old days, at times of trial such as these, any enemy of Jupiter Latiaris would have been ceremonially burnt at the stake. Diana would have demanded her share of the sacrifices as well. How awesome is Diana! From Tauris to Nemi she causes blood to boil. Priest, perform your duties!

FIRST COMMONER: Carmenta has prophesied the triumph of Rome. Death to Carmenta!

SECOND COMMONER: Any friend of Rome should be put to death today.

ANTISTIUS: You invoke the justice of the gods against your enemies through horrifying crimes which would revolt any reasonably moral person. Heavens above! What perverse notions you have of your deity to believe she can be appeased by such abominations!

DOLABELLA: We have no more need of your reasoning. We practise our ancestral rites. What gives you the right to think you can change them?

ANTISTIUS: By the same right our ancestors had to initiate them. I am doing away with all the filthy blemishes a barbarous age introduced to the ancient mysteries. I'm getting rid of the deformations, the excrescences which have become attached to our sacred rites. Our original religion has been distorted by constant innovations, vile transformations which threaten to destroy it. As for our rites, you believe that something which has been practised for but a few years must come from time immemorial. And anyone like me who attempts to purge the impurities is considered an innovator.

METIUS: This is the very reason why one should never get involved with religion, Liberalis. Belief can't stand still, it changes constantly over the years and people must practise as they find it in their own time.

ANTISTIUS: *(mortified)* Oh, how hard it is to lie unless you are a habitual liar!

FIRST COMMONER: Enough! We can't go to war without a priest to bless us. That's like going on a voyage without consulting an augury, or building a house without conforming to the sacred geometry. We want a new priest! Give us a new priest!

NARRATOR: LIBERALIS *and others surround* ANTISTIUS *and drag him away.*

VOICES: We want a new priest! Give us a new priest!

SCENE SEVEN.

NARRATOR: *In his house* METIUS *meets with* LIBERALIS.

METIUS: Please, Liberalis, you must not consider my actions to be motivated by blind passions of the aristocratic class. I love the people quite as much as you – the difference is I know their limitations far better than you do. Your mistake is that you don't understand that human affairs are petty, stupid even, nothing to do with any idealism. Each of us is circumscribed by the portion of light which has been granted to us. And only the nobility have been granted the possession of intelligence and virtue. The common folk have every right to be immoral. I'll go further: the immorality of the populace is what guarantees our liberty. As long as the people dance and sing and drink we remain free.

My views on religion are not unlike yours, the difference being that I'm wiser than you. I say nothing; I keep apart from the fray. The masses need religion and it's up to the state to allow them that consolation. The state should ensure the people have the kind of priests they demand. Antistius has got above himself. That man has never understood what is expected of a priest. In the order of things appearance is all. What counts is not what he believes but how the common herd expect him to act. You can't play with the feelings of the people without them realising what's going on. Poor Antistius! Should anyone kill him he will only have himself to blame – he will as good as killed himself.

LIBERALIS: It's true he makes too few concessions to human folly. But the spiritual sentiments of the populace rarely have much foresight. We need to make the people accept what we know to be good for them – which is so often the opposite of what they think they want. This an internal problem, don't complicate it by an external war. After all, today's ceremony went off well enough. If we continue to give Antistius support then the people will come to consider him every bit as legitimate as his predecessors, those assassins. Weren't you moved by the sincerity of his patriotism and by the enthusiasm for Latium which breathes through all Carmenta's oracles?

METIUS: You're confusing the issue. There are two kinds of patriotism: one big and one small. Certainly Antistius has a loyalty for the Latin peoples – well, for the whole of humanity, you might say. But he has no loyalty to Alba. He's a wise man, a philosopher, a humanitarian… but he's a dreamer. He sees a great future for the whole of the Latin race – an empire without frontiers; but he has no feeling for his own Alban people. Our ancestors, the founders of Alba, never had such lofty ideas – the safety of the city was enough for them to care about. In those days the Sibyl had a narrower horizon, she only uttered prophecies that were in the interests of Alba.

LIBERALIS: Why do you think patriotism is a straitjacket? Can you deny that Antistius is a fine citizen? Only those whose patriotism consists of drumming up hatred towards Rome and the Romans could consider him a traitor.

METIUS: What makes you think I'm not smart enough to see that? Have you ever heard me publicly speak wrong of that excellent man? I think too well of him. But no-one should ever consider himself too perfect to connect with the masses; above all, to deign to speak to the people in a language they don't understand. Antistius, for all his fine qualities, has caused more grief to the fatherland than the worst villain. Because of him the temple of Nemi, our national shrine, has become a sanctuary for cowards. It does no good to mess around with popular sentiment, because it's built on shaky foundations. Antistius is asking for a hero's death by cutting away the very roots of heroism. Antistius is every bit as dangerous as the demagogue Cethegus and his crew, who every day stab at the heart of our land, who would destroy our green oaks and tear down our walls. He's a menace. I hate him to the core and depth of my soul.

LIBERALIS: Then take it all the way. Pay someone to kill him.

METIUS: No need of that. Whenever there's a crime that needs to be committed you can always find someone to do it gratis.

NARRATOR: *A noise from without and the* SERVANT *enters.*

SERVANT: My lords, there's a great commotion among the people. Gangs are marching to Nemi. They're saying they're going to kill the false priest and restore the old customs so the goddess might be propitious in the coming war. Casca and Latro are with them. Your lordships know that whenever those miscreants are involved it'll end in bloodshed.

METIUS: The gods use strange instruments to satisfy their ends. After all, they do whatsoever is their will.

NARRATOR: LIBERALIS h*ears terrible cries from without and leaves.*

METIUS: *(cont. aside)* The affairs of state are beginning to return to order. The world will once again lie down in its proper bed – the bed of transgression. What fond illusion of ludicrous fanatics like those two to imagine humanity can go through life without violence, that reason can rule the world. As if men were rational beings! It's the expedient crime that makes the world turn. In these difficult times Liberalis knows nothing of how to make the people dance to his tune. He supposes he governs by popular mandate, but the people will never follow such as him. His own army is not even on his side. Will Liberalis even be able to save Antistius?

SCENE EIGHT.

NARRATOR: METIUS *goes outside to join* LIBERALIS. *They hear voices from the* CROWD.

A VOICE FROM THE CROWD: *(off-stage)* Antistius is slain! Casca has killed him! The false priest is no more!

SECOND VOICE: Blessed be the blade which has killed the false priest. Now our victory is certain.

THIRD VOICE: Now once again will religion flourish. Religion is the measure of a nation's strength.

MATERNA: His death was well deserved. He refused to save my son.

LIBERALIS: This is the reward of spiritual integrity and righteousness. We shall not see the like of such a reforming priest again, Metius.

METIUS: So much the better! You should never have encouraged such a revolutionary.

LIBERALIS: You prefer to encourage iniquity? Carry on then, but beware of what will pass through the gate you've opened.

METIUS: Most amusing! Oh heavens, how wrong can you be! It's your own supporters who've done the killing. You flatter yourself that you lead these people, but what defines them is their very resistance to being led. I won't hold you responsible for their crimes; but don't have the nerve to blame me for them. Public opinion demands a punishment for every crime. *Is fecit cui podest*: the one who did it is the one who profits.

LIBERALIS: It's you who will profit from Casca's crime.

METIUS: My god, how? The present situation means no-one benefits and everyone suffers.

NARRATOR: VOLTINIUS *comes over.*

VOLTINIUS: You used these wretches, Metius!

METIUS: Never! This was a spontaneous manifestation of the popular will. You should always respect and never try to analyse motives which drive a mob to massacre, Voltinius. These people have nothing but their patriotism. Leave them to worship their false gods.

VOLTINIUS: How come you're so tolerant of these murderous wretches?

METIUS: When our country is at stake these are the victims who lay down their lives. They're worth far more than your tavern brawlers and street-corner orators. They do what they can. In great public disputes everyone must join in according to their station. Society is like a teeming anthill.

Those who know only how to massacre must massacre.

VOLTINIUS: Crime is always crime.

METIUS: Oh, you poor little innocent. You know nothing of what it means to be born to rule. Ponder on the oracle of Jupiter Latiaris: *Regere imperio populos* – rule the people by might! The ignorant are governed by an appreciation of their weaknesses, their need to be fooled, flattered, spun around like some brainless Cyclops, some blind force rushing around like a mad bull. Now and then among such dimwits you might possibly find one good citizen… or I should say, someone who believes himself to be one. In this state of grand illusion who is right and who is wrong?

Listen to these muffled cries – they're getting closer. Make sense of them if you can. Some are howling, some are mewling, some are crying, some are praying. The mob is like a sharpened sword on the march and woe unto anyone who gets in the way.

NARRATOR: *The CROWD arrives bearing CASCA in triumph, he brandishes a blood-stained dagger. GANEO follows.*

GANEO: I always said it would end badly. I've been proved right today. I want power because it's said power expands, enlarges and enhances a man. We shall see.

FIRST CITIZEN: Order will be restored. I move that the name of Antistius be scrubbed off the honourable record of the priests of Nemi.

SECOND CITIZEN: Quite right. But who will be now take the role of priest?

THIRD CITIZEN: Yes, the false priest is slain, but the true

priest… Who will he be?

FOURTH CITIZEN: Yes, who? Tetricus is dead.

FIRST CITIZEN: By rights it should be Casca. He has slain his predecessor.

SECOND CITIZEN: Casca! You must be joking!

FIRST CITIZEN: No, that's the custom. Casca killed the Priest. Now he should be priest in his turn.

THIRD CITIZEN: That's certain. Casca has become the true Priest of Nemi according to the rite of succession.

FOURTH CITIZEN: My faith, he's as good as any other!

SECOND CITIZEN: He's a villain!

FIRST CITIZEN: Priesthood and personal worth have nothing in common.

NARRATOR: METIUS *comes forward to address the crowd*:

METIUS: Citizens, at last we have a priest according to our ancient custom. Now let's be calm. Victory over Rome is certain.

NARRATOR: *The criminal* LATRO *approaches* CASCA.

LATRO: Well, comrade, seems as if you'll be priest. Fair enough. But never forget, Casca, I was there with you when you did it. It could just as well have been me who struck the blow!

CASCA: All right, Latro, take it easy. You'll be taken good care of.

LATRO: 'Take it easy.' Is that all you've got to say?

CASCA: *(aside)* So, this fool's already plotting to become my successor. It'd take no more than one thrust of his dagger... and he has so many lives on his conscience already. *(out loud)* I'm telling you, take it easy, Latro.

LATRO: Okay, I'll take it easy, Casca... for today.

CASCA: *(aside)* Cursèd custom! Hardly guaranteed to lead to golden slumbers for the High Priest!

NARRATOR: *The* CROWD *assembles before the Forum. Sacrificial* VICTIMS *are led to the front of the Temple.* METIUS *takes* CASCA *to one side.*

METIUS: Well, well, Casca. So now you're the priest. This is not the time for a long conversation – we're being watched, though no-one can hear us. I'll back your claim to priesthood, but you're nobody's fool. You know very well that I could just as well supply a successor any moment.

CASCA: A successor? But the ancient rule has been restored.

METIUS: Exactly! You're a dyed-in-the-wool villain who has deserved death twenty times over because of your crimes. You know better than anyone how swift a death blow can be dealt. There's more than one who wouldn't think twice about assuming the robes of priesthood of Nemi with such little effort.

CASCA: Your lordship will surely be satisfied with me. I'd be the biggest fool around if I didn't fulfil the duties of the priesthood to the letter.

METIUS: We'll start with the lists of the human sacrifices to

Jupiter Latiaris. I'll draw up those lists myself. No-one must be allowed to add or remove a single name. Understand?

CASCA: That's settled, your lordship. What about my mate Latro, for instance?

METIUS: We shall see.

CASCA: Ah! That'll depend on what the Sibyl has to say, eh?

METIUS: *(aside)* I've done well. This is the price that had to be paid for the future of Alba. The people were going soft, on the road to ruin. They were coming to believe that human justice is superior to the implacable will of the gods. I have restored the ancient custom. By reinstating sacrifice I can get rid of the treacherous leaders of the subversive factions, both liberals and demagogues, at a stroke. How can society thrive without human sacrifice? Those who disagree can go and swell the ranks of those Roman bandits they admire so much.

NARRATOR: *The* BOURGEOISIE *surround* METIUS.

FIRST BOURGEOIS: How fine are these old customs of ours!

SECOND BOURGEOIS: Lesser minds could never comprehend their philosophical profundity.

FIRST BOURGEOIS: The independence of the priest must be guaranteed. The priest deserves a high temporal position.

SECOND BOURGEOIS: But the priest must be protected from his own weakness.

METIUS: That's what I call right-thinking. You want to be protected from your own weakness, don't you, Casca?

CASCA: Yes, your lordship.

METIUS: *(aside)* He's like some clapped-out seventy year-old whore who's sold herself to the whole world and who now protests: 'Save me from my weakness!' This is what the priesthood has come to! *(out loud)* Citizens, now deliver yourselves to that great joy which is so well warranted by the glad tidings of this great day. Casca is the true priest. He has killed his predecessor. *Ecce sacerdos magnus.* Behold the High Priest!

NARRATOR: VIRGINIUS *and* VIRGINIA *have been watching sadly.*

VIRGINIUS: Our poor priest Antistius! In this world when a man has principles he has to hide his true feelings or come to nought.

VIRGINIA: He should have been content to confide the truth to we who would listen.

FIRST BOURGEOIS: How great it is to feel that our faith is restored, that the old order is rebuilt upon time-honoured foundations! Contemptible Antistius was the cause of all our woes. Now we have a true pontiff, who has killed his predecessor according to the custom. He did the right thing, because that predecessor was despicable.

SECOND BOURGEOIS: What a great consolation. As far as I'm concerned, it's as if I'm breathing fresh air again. What a great calamity it was for us to have a false priest!

FIRST BOURGEOIS: From this moment on I reckon Rome is as good as defeated. A false city with a false creed and false priests – that's what I think of Rome. This would be a great time to bring King Priscus back from the Hernicians!

SECOND BOURGEOIS: Better wait a while. That would be too much to expect. Priscus cannot return to take his seat upon the throne until he can reign over a people worthy of him. When the people are ready, then we'll bring back Priscus.

FIRST BOURGEOIS: That might take some time.

SECOND BOURGEOIS: All our best customs have been restored. When the rites are reverenced in the proper manner the gods will be satisfied. The life of the world depends upon long-practised traditions.

FIRST BOURGEOIS: Soon we shall bring back again the sacrifices to Jupiter Latiaris.

SECOND BOURGEOIS: How blessed we are! The gods, the family and private property... all saved by one stroke of the sword! Once again will faith flourish. All trace of progress will soon be eradicated. The great customs of the Latin kings will again be observed forever.

FIRST BOURGEOIS: Holy, happy day! How fortunate are those of us here to witness it! And to say that all this came to pass because of a shameful madman. Still, when the beast died his poison died with him. Days like this really count in the life of a people! They are bought only at the cost of tainted blood.

SECOND BOURGEOIS: Today is the day of universal reconciliation. Truly Antistius has been the victim of our people's salvation.

NARRATOR: *Cries of joy as tables are laid and the flesh of sacrificial animals is served... But then CARMENTA arrives in her black dress and with dishevelled hair. She goes straight up to* CASCA.

CARMENTA: So, Casca, I hear it is you who are now the true priest of Nemi?

CASCA: That's right. It's me.

CARMENTA: *(with a ferocious laugh)* Then this is for you, my priest! Antistius, I avenge you!

NARRATOR: *She strikes* CASCA *in the heart with a dagger; he falls.*

FIRST CITIZEN: Traitress! All is lost! One hour of peace… Now a new abyss.

SECOND CITIZEN: How terrible! When all was going so well!

CARMENTA: Hearken unto the voice of the Sibyl! Far, far in the distance I see him appear. I have seen his face but I know not his name. I have seen the prophecy written in letters I comprehend not. I have seen his star rising in the east. Nine times more shall the just man be slaughtered. But on the tenth time his tomb shall be the site of glory. For a God will come to judge the earth. Good will vanquish Evil. Those who abhor altars dripping with the blood of beasts and men will be born again to bliss everlasting in the bosom of the great eternal God who will bring forth a host of witnesses to truth, clad in robes of white. Tremble with joy, you who will be martyred in his name, for your blood will not be spilled in vain. Do not seek to dry the fountain of tears, for God will spring forth from our lamentations.

From this hour the future belongs to Rome. Alba will be forgotten… ancient history. No-one will even know where once this city stood. Now it is your turn to avenge the blood of your Priest. Kill the Sibyl of Latium. I offer you my breast. Strike!

NARRATOR: *She sees the blood on her hands and uncovers her breast. No-one moves. She leaves. The crowd parts in silence to let her pass.*

TITIUS: There cannot be the same Sibyl for two succeeding priests. The prophetess poses even more danger than Antistius. How could Casca have let that woman live?

FIRST CITIZEN: He must have taken pity on her. The imbecile!

TITIUS: She should have been slain along with Antistius.

SECOND CITIZEN: That would have availed us nothing. The voice of the Sibyl lives forever. Such creatures never die. That's what gives them their mystery. There will always be a Sibyl.

DOLABELLA: We have to stop her.

METIUS: No! Leave her be. She's nothing without her Priest and Antistius is dead. We'll hear no more of her tomorrow.

LATRO: My Lord Metius, are you intending to appoint a replacement? Look no further. You see, I'm here, ready and waiting. It could have been me who became the legitimate Priest. I was every bit as ready to kill Antistius. I was Casca's side-kick. I'm just as good as he was. Better. Come on, you all know I'm destined to be the successor!

NARRATOR: HERDONIUS *arrives breathless.*

HERDONIUS: I come from Rome with portentous news.

Romulus has murdered Remus. The augury has come to pass: the establishment of the city has been consummated by fratricide. The blood of brothers creates the prophesied foundation.

FIRST CITIZEN: What an awesome day. A city founded on fratricide. And a malefactor takes on the role of priest to safeguard, so we're told, our city. The ways of the world are enough to confound the mind of man.

SECOND CITIZEN: All is shrouded in mystery. Who can interpret such obscurities? Not for nothing is old Janus two-faced. The world goes forth through the hatred of two hostile brothers!

THIRD CITIZEN: May the will of the gods be accomplished.

FIRST CITIZEN: May the good laws of the Latin kings flourish eternally in our mountains and groves!

NARRATOR: *A hollow, terrifying voice is heard, that of a captive* PROPHET OF ISRAEL.

PROPHET OF ISRAEL: Thus saith the Lord of Hosts: The walls shall be utterly broken and the high gates shall be burned with fire; and the people shall labour in vain, and the folk in the fire, and they shall be weary.

(Jeremiah LI, 58)

THE PRIEST OF NEMI – THE END.